16x 6/00 ✓ 7/00
24x 11/01 (12/01)
38x 3/07 ✓ 7/07

LJ

8/97

PROVENCE:
THE ART OF LIVING

Foreword by Terence Conran

Photographs by Sølvi Dos Santos

Text by Sara Walden

Stewart, Tabori & Chang
New York

Contents

— 7 —

Foreword by Sir Terence Conran

— 9 —

Introduction

— 13 —

Tradition and Renewal

— 97 —

Exuberant Creativity

— 195 —

Guide

— 205 —

Index

— 207 —

Acknowledgements

My love-affair with France has lasted some forty years or more, and she's proved a very constant companion. For ten years now, I have owned a house in Provence, where I retire to work in peace, drink in the sun and satiate my appetite on the wonderfully aromatic fresh produce and crisp local wine.

In spite of the blistering sun and the fearsome *mistral*, Provence is an outdoor place in all but the depths of winter. The vernacular architecture does a wonderful job of keeping the interiors cool while—in the country at least—opening up the houses to the world outside. Traditionally the exteriors are covered with *crépi*, a rendering that weathers and blisters over the years as it bakes beneath the summer sun. *Crépi* is coloured using natural pigments that complement and add to the color of the countryside: those characteristic blue shutters whose color is supposed to keep out the insects; the rust-red and geranium-pink of traditional farmhouses; the cool, thick whitewash of the Côte d'Azur.

These fantastic colours you find—diverse but never garish—change quite dramatically over the course of a single day. The summer may bring a seemingly endless succession of sunny days, but they are anything other than monotonous. The extraordinary quality of the light casts its magic across town and country alike. Fierce and unforgiving at midday, it bleaches all but the strongest colors; later, as the afternoon gently wanes into evening, a mellowing silver light filters through the olive groves and cypress trees, and the landscape is suspended in an ethereal calm, the peace broken only by the crickets, toads and cicadas, and the buzz of hopeful mosquitoes.

Terence Conran

"One would never have a house that looked like this anywhere else in the world." So declares Sarah St. George of her traditional Provençal farmhouse, solidly sober on the outside, inside a dazzling extravaganza of abstract patterns inspired largely by African art. It is only one of a cornucopia of fine buildings representing Provence's rich architectural heritage—elegant villas on the languorous Côte d'Azur; rustic village houses in the mountainous, aromatic hinterland; patrician *mas*, or farmhouses, set among vineyards and lavender fields; converted barns and grand *bastides*—which within these pages open their doors to reveal a profusion of exhilarating surprises. It becomes abundantly clear that a glorious alchemy is at work, by which the celebrated exuberance of Provence's natural colors and light combine with the passions and expertise of its inhabitants to produce interiors of striking originality.

Intimacy and authenticity, comfort and charm are the hallmarks of these interiors: they are not lavish backdrops to luxurious lifestyles, nor self-conscious pastiches of "Provençal" style. If some are the creations of today's most acclaimed designers it is because they are their own much-loved homes or country retreats. Lived in and very personal, each of these homes expresses a unique vision and aesthetic. Enthusiasts all, the owners combine their special passions—from antique textiles to folk art, from gastronomy to *haute couture*—with a shared delight in and understanding of their native or adopted pays.

This magical land is universally associated with sensuous colors that spring not from the conceit of any designer but from the earth. Provence is also deeply enduring, over the centuries absorbing what suited it from waves of different influences—Greek, Roman, Spanish, Indian, English, to name but a few—and proudly withstanding the rest. Breathtaking use of color and audacious eclecticism are

thus not surprisingly among the keynotes struck by these interiors. Fired by the legendary southern light, Michel Klein, prodigy of French fashion design, has painted his sixteenth-century farmhouse in a vivid palette and filled it with furnishings of diverse styles and eras that nevertheless agree in terms of sensibility. Irène and Giorgio Silvagni have translated their passion for the visual and graphic arts—he as a film producer, she as a former editor of French *Vogue*—into an intense love affair with their Renaissance house, long abandoned yet now ablaze with pigments applied with considerable *éclat*. In Arles, on the fringes of the Camargue, Anne Igou has restored the Grand Hôtel Nord-Pinus—haunt of Hemingway, Picasso, Cocteau and generations of proud matadors—to its former glory, a fitting setting for a Christian Lacroix fashion show vibrant with Provençal colors: poppy scarlet, sunflower gold, grape violet.

Serendipity is raised to an art form by Jacques Grange, the most sought-after interior decorator in France and a magician of effortless style. In his converted barn colors are ordained by the light and the surrounding countryside, while the eclectic contents supply the element of surprise that is his trademark. In Marie-Stella Castanier's converted barn near Avignon ethnic influences predominate, her own largely Mexican-inspired designs blending seamlessly with what she regards as the ethos of Provence: simple, unpretentious, generous and authentic.

As well as kindling such exuberant creativity, Provence can also foster grandiose fantasies. The dramatic arrangements conceived by Sacha and Lionel Houant in their Lubéron farmhouse, for example, set against backdrops of startling blues and Pompeiian-inspired frescoes, resemble nothing so much as fantastical stage sets. Tania Vartan's Riviera villa is a rococo confection of trompe-l'œil and fantasy finishes, inspired by the Italian Renaissance and the palaces of Europe. And in their hunting lodge set in an ornamental landscape of gardens, fountains and grottoes, Lillian Williams and her husband dedicate themselves and their home to recapturing in minute detail the life and fugitive spirit of eighteenth-century France.

It has been said that in Provence "austerity and gentleness confront and complement each other", and it comes as no surprise that this land of sublime paradoxes and fierce extremes should also inspire visions of authenticity and simplicity, shading occasionally into austerity. Understated elegance is the essence of Hélène Lafforgue's *chambres d'hôtes*, as it is of embroiderer Edith Mézard's classical eighteenth-century château. Aesthetic rigor distinguishes Xavier Nicod's uncompromising, uncluttered approach to the restoration of his 600-year-old village house, tempered with tenderness in the decor of a baby's bedroom. Purism also characterizes the village house—furnished with favorite pieces all "bought for thruppence" at local markets—and garden of Nicole de Vésian, a former consultant for Hermès, which in their ruggedness echo the Lubéron mountain range in whose shadow they lie.

More rural simplicity is found in artist Joe Downing's intriguing complex of four seventeenth-century cottages and two grottoes, while a cloistered calm safeguards the monastic isolation of gourmet *par excellence* Richard Olney in his minimally restored village retreat near Toulon, the embodiment of his mantra, "Keep it simple, simple, simple." Rigor of a more scholarly kind defines Hannelore and Achim Stein's restoration of the Hôtel de la Mirande in Avignon, a tireless quest for absolute authenticity involving long-forgotten building techniques and recuperated materials. Every pane of glass is handblown, wallpapers are faithful copies of eighteenth-century handblocked designs, and many of the objects have stories to tell of previous lives elsewhere.

Provence has long enjoyed a particular affinity with artists and writers: Van Gogh, Matisse, Cézanne, Chagall, Picasso, Pagnol, Giono and Mistral, among many others, all found inspiration here. This book is both an evocation and a celebration of the extraordinary spirit of creativity that is unmistakably still alive today. Within these private worlds fashioned by a galaxy of creative talents, the traditions and lore of the old Provence and the spirit of the new unite in an enchanting harmony. Each of these worlds is wholly individual, but they are bound by common threads; of aesthetic originality; of respect for what has gone before; above all, of a passion for the textures and colors of what the writer Alphonse Daudet hauntingly described as that land "born of the sun; it lives by light".

Tradition
and Renewal

*F*rench

lovers of Provence are not content

merely to respect and

preserve the traditions of the past.

They recreate and enrich them

—and by so doing are enriched themselves.

*A*bove: The dining room where Hélène's guests enjoy their breakfasts is a wonderful sun-filled space. The Provençal *buffet* is eighteenth-century, and the old table's top has been painted with the pigments of Ventoux.

Right: The floors of the Mas de l'Ange would have needed 300 square yards of tiles; to economize, they were made of cement dyed various colors then studded with lozenge-shaped stones. No two rooms have the same pattern of pebbles embedded in their floors.

HOMAGE TO NATURAL STYLE

Under a majestic archway of plane trees—planted, it is said, to provide shade for Napoleon's armies—the road from St-Rémy-de-Provence passes through Mollégès, which was once an important staging post on the journey to Cavaillon, where Hélène Lafforgue was born. Just off that regal road, in a delightful garden complete with a tranquil pond, there now stands the Mas de l'Ange. *A chambres d'hôtes* that she runs with her husband, Bruno, it is an object lesson in what can be achieved when a farmhouse built without much imagination in the 1930s is transformed with instinctive flair.

Hélène, who comes from old Provençal stock, works for a French interior design magazine and is also a stylist in her own right, with a genius for understated elegance inherited from her mother. Her best ideas are those of pure simplicity.

Each of the five guest bedrooms is given an individual character by the sensitive use of colors, planned around the fabrics and furniture they contain: one predominantly white, one rose, one a warm yellow, another crisply blue and white, another the seductive gray-greens of celadon porcelain. They are decorated with fine antiques, and made intimate by the liberal scattering of cherished personal belongings: a straw hat balanced on the corner of a picture frame, a pair of espadrilles left dangling over a door, photograph-albums strewn on a chair—anything that might imply that this is a home rather than a hotel. Each room has its own white-tiled bathroom lit naturally through skylights in the roof. The cement floors are washed in shades that match the decor.

Downstairs, in what was once the tractor shed, a painting of a voluptuous nude presides over the living-cum-breakfast room; splashes of ocher, red and green are applied with great subtlety—in pottery, in quilts tumbling out of an old wood armoire, in warm-toned glassware. The floor is another stroke of ingenuity. Faced with the daunting task of covering some 300 square yards, the Lafforgues opted again for cement, this time dyed a deep ocher yellow and, as in the bedrooms, studded with small stones in intricate inlaid patterns, no two of which are the same.

Outside, blue-gray shutters are half-closed against the sunlight, and—more often than not—one of Bruno's horses peers sleepily out over the stable door. The overall effect is of an affectionate home waiting to welcome not customers but friends.

*A*BOVE: A SADDLE RESTS ON A SADDLE RACK, UNDER PAINTINGS OF WOMEN IN PROVENÇAL DRESS. ON THE CHEST A BUST FACES THE MORNING LIGHT AND AN ANTIQUE MIRROR IS UPTURNED TOWARDS THE WHITEWASHED CEILING.

BELOW: WARM YELLOWS ARE A RECURRING THEME IN THE MAS DE L'ANGE. HERE, A TABLE MADE OF BRANCHES, BEARING A BRANCH LAMP WITH A YELLOW SHADE, STANDS BY A DAY BED COVERED IN OCHER FABRIC. TWO ANTIQUE TOY HORSES PREPARE TO CHARGE ON ONE OF THE HOUSE'S FEW TILE-COVERED FLOORS.

RIGHT: THE SOFA AND CHAIRS IN THE FAMILY'S LIVING ROOM ARE FROM ST-RÉMY. A CAST-IRON CHANDELIER HANGS ABOVE A LOW TABLE—ORIGINALLY A KITCHEN TABLE—WHOSE LEGS HAVE BEEN SHORTENED. WHEREVER THE LINES OF SMALL RIVER PEBBLES INTERSECT IN THE FLOOR, SLIGHTLY LARGER STONES ARE EMBEDDED.

$\mathscr{A}$BOVE: IN THE KITCHEN, WHERE HÉLÈNE'S AND BRUNO'S TWO YOUNG DAUGHTERS DO THEIR HOMEWORK, A COLLECTION OF ANTIQUE GLASSES AND GLASS DECANTERS IS DISPLAYED ON A PAINTED WOODEN CUPBOARD.

RIGHT: THE DESK WHERE HÉLÈNE WORKS IS IN THE FAMILY'S TRANQUIL LIVING ROOM. A LADDER LEANS ON FLOOR-TO-CEILING SHELVES BUILT BY BRUNO.

*A*bove: The "white" guest bedroom is a homage to natural materials. Rough unbleached cloth has been used as a bed cover. The eighteenth-century mirror, off-white ceiling and walls evenly distribute soft light from a low window.

Below: In the "yellow" bedroom, twin wooden beds with a handpainted floral design, and plump comforters in the light-absorbing color of sunflowers, invite you to slumber.

Right: A fragile old table found in a flea market near St-Rémy has been restored to elegance thanks to Hélène's care. The bowl in varnished clay is from L'Autre Côté in Avignon. Loops and twirls of river stones seem to dance on the smooth cement floor.

*A*bove: A *boutis* quilt
flows from the mouth of an olive oil
jar in a corner of the Silvagni's salon.
Right: In the garden Irène likes to
collect sweet-smelling plants and cac-
ti on an old iron table. "Everything
that grows is a pleasure," she says.

RESTORATION DRAMA

A jewel of a house, the home of Irène and Giorgio Silvagni dates from the Renaissance; rebuilt in 1665, it is near the *mas* where Molière was married. It had stood empty for 100 years when they came to Provence, feeling the need to put down anchor. They chanced upon it one weekend, bought it within a week, and so embarked on a heady love affair. At the slightest excuse Irène, the former editor of French *Vogue*, abandons Paris to head south, and as soon as she draws near: "My heart beats faster..." For Giorgio, producer of what he calls "difficult" films—masterpieces like *Le Bal* and *Z* and, most recently, *Ulysses' Gaze*—the house is a living thing: changing, strong-willed, capricious even, for it rejects furniture it does not like.

A labor of intense love, restoring the house took them two years. The fine furniture and paintings that they brought down from Paris were promptly removed by burglars so they began again, often buying pieces from the local demolition man and faithfully reviving them. Now every beautifully proportioned room contains something magical: an ocher-painted chest of drawers that the house has definitely accepted; beds that were sofas and sofas that are now beds; portly bathtubs on legs, complete with brass showerheads; antique linens and fabulous fabrics unearthed in markets.

A source of immense pride, Irène has created her first garden, filled with white geraniums, vervain and citronella; with roses growing over a bower and morning glory winding its way up the walls of the house: a medley of blue and white with splashes of yellow.

Giorgio, meanwhile, is ever busy with new masterpieces, painting the walls of each room, frequenting a long-established shop in Paris for special pigments that the house will welcome: pale green for the guest bedroom, with a frieze of fern-like fronds to complement a delicate flower painted in the window embrasure; ochre for the kitchen walls, otherwise tiled purely in white; oxblood red for the dining room, where red and gold threaded saris from India are looped over black metal pelmets that Giorgio designed. His *coup d'éclat* is surely the living room, where two small fountains are set into alcoves, and where the walls flame an astonishing crimson red. In the early evenings, when the rays of the sunset stream through the windows, it seems as though the room—like the Silvagnis' passion for their house—is ablaze.

LEFT: HEAVY, EMBROIDERED FELT CURTAINS CONCEAL A WINDOW AT ONE END OF THE DINING ROOM. NONE OF THE CHINA IN THE HOUSE IS PURELY FOR SHOW, NOT EVEN THE DIEULEFIT AND VALLAURIS POTTERY ON THE SHELVES. THE SINK BELOW, WHERE IRÈNE CUTS THE FLOWERS SHE ARRANGES, IS ORIGINAL TO THE HOUSE.

RIGHT: DURING THE REVOLUTION *LANTERNES RÉVOLUTIONNAIRES*—WITH CANDLE FLAMES FLICKERING BEHIND RED, WHITE AND BLUE GLASS—WERE CARRIED THROUGH THE STREETS: THE CHANDELIER IN THE DINING ROOM IS THE ADAPTED FRAME OF ONE SUCH LANTERN. THE PORTRAIT SHOWS GIORGIO'S GREAT-GRANDMOTHER, PAOLINA. THE SOFA DATES FROM THE END OF THE NINETEENTH CENTURY BUT IS COVERED WITH A 1940s SCARLET AND ORANGE *COUVERTURE PIQUÉE*. THE SILVAGNIS MADE THE CONSOLE TABLE BY PLACING A SEMICIRCLE OF FAKE MARBLE ON TOP OF AN OLD BALCONY RAIL.

*L*EFT: THE *CALADE* FLOOR IN THE SALON, WITH RIVER STONES THICKLY EMBEDDED IN CEMENT, IS A COMMON SIGHT IN THE STREETS AND COURTYARDS OF MEDITERRANEAN COUNTRIES. THE SILVAGNIS WANTED THEIRS TO LOOK "RATHER ROUGH", LIKE THE SQUARES IN PROVENCE. THE SIDES OF A BED-CUM-SOFA ARE COVERED WITH MATTRESS TICKING BOUGHT FROM THE MARCHÉ ST PIERRE IN PARIS FOR THE BARGAIN PRICE OF 20 FRANCS A YARD.

ABOVE: A NINETEENTH-CENTURY BUREAU, PAINTED BLACK BY GIORGIO, BEARS A LARGE PROVENÇAL *JARRE*, ASHTRAYS FOUND IN THE LEBANON AND AFGHANISTAN AND A KITSCH JAPANESE FACE MADE OF PLASTER.

BELOW: GIORGIO AND IRÈNE OFTEN WORK OPPOSITE EACH OTHER AT A SMALL OVAL TABLE IN A CORNER OF THEIR BEDROOM. AS IT HAS NEVER BEEN UPHOLSTERED, THE 1930S VIENNESE SOFA IS CASUALLY DRAPED WITH A FAVORITE PIECE OF FABRIC.

*L*EFT: GIORGIO PAINTED THE BATHROOM WALLS TO RESEMBLE BIG TILES, IN A TROMPE-L'OEIL EFFECT. HE ALSO PAINTED THE PLUMP OLD BATHTUB, AND DESIGNED THE PELMET.

RIGHT: WHEN SHE VISITS THEM, IRÈNE'S AND GIORGIO'S DAUGHTER SLEEPS IN A HIGH BED, MADE BY A *MENUISIER* AND COVERED IN ANTIQUE LINEN AND A *COUVERTURE PIQUÉE*, IN A ROOM THAT WAS ONCE A STABLE. AN ANTIQUE CONSOLE TABLE STANDS AT ITS HEAD. SET INTO THE "MATISSE BLUE" WALLS ARE THE FORMER LIVING QUARTERS OF PIGEONS AND (BELOW) A SMALL ALCOVE.

MAGICAL REALISM

In a dazzling career that has made him the most celebrated interior decorator in France—and a celebrity in his own right—Jacques Grange has acquired the reputation of a magician: the creator of an unpretentious style that is so abbreviated that it appears entirely effortless. To create his own magical home in Provence—a low-lying drystone barn set in the grounds of an eighteenth-century château —he insists he used no more than "three bolts of fabric and a lick of paint". There was, of course, rather more to it than that.

The colors of the house were ordained by the mass of greenery that clings to the ocher-rose façade, and by the ever-changing influences of the extraordinary light. On the ground floor the hues are *faux blanc*, blue-green or "an eighteenth-century yellow", with the ceilings washed in honey-beige. Upstairs the bedrooms have been imbued with what Jacques calls "an Italian pink", and "the blue of tears". Floors are terracotta or a green-yellow. The shutters are sienna.

Furniture and furnishings are entirely eclectic and their selection capricious, for it is an essential part of Jacques' ethos, and his success, to mix the unexpected. In the large sun-drenched living room, for example, a 1950s carved oak table by Jean Royère is complemented by an oversized tripod table chosen because 'it looks like the one in Matisse's *Les Capucines à La Danse*. A simple rush-bottomed chair 'just like the one from Van Gogh's bedroom' (in *The Artist's Bedroom at Arles*) mixes happily with much more modern versions by Charlotte Perriand, a delicate Louis XIII *fauteuil* and luxurious contemporary sofas. Basket-woven bulls' heads hang from an upright wooden coat-rack because they remind him of one he saw in a photograph of Picasso's studio. Since it is also part of Jacques' genius to provide surprise, an almost life-size metal bull—*a toro de fuego*—stands by the window, fitted with a traditional comic mask from the Camargue.

Jacques escapes to the house from Paris at Christmas and Easter, and for long weekends in the summer, when, surrounded by friends, he basks "like a lizard" in an idyllic garden where almost every vista reveals a scene that was the original inspiration for a painting by Van Gogh. This is where he finds the calming rhythm that his life now requires. It is his "house of utter happiness", the only place where he can imagine the pleasures of growing old.

*L*EFT: IN THE KITCHEN FLEA-
MARKET CHAIRS ARE GROUPED AROUND A
TABLE SET WITH A CHECKERED TABLECLOTH
AND EARTHENWARE FOUND LOCALLY. AN
OPEN SHELF BOASTS A COLLECTION OF
1930S BOWLS AND GLASSES.

ABOVE: A GROUND-FLOOR BEDROOM DIS-
PLAYS A SIMILAR HAPPY MIXTURE OF STYLES,
BUT ALSO A COMMON DENOMINATOR:
GREEN. A WHITE MOSQUITO NET GATHERED
ABOVE THE BED ABSORBS THE VARYING
SHADES OF THE DOORS, WOODEN CHAIR AND
PISTACHIO QUILT. PANELS OF FABRIC PAINT-
ED BY BOISSEAU HANG FROM THE WALLS.

*L*EFT: IN THE LIVING ROOM—ONCE A SHED FOR FARM ANIMALS—BERBER RUGS FROM THE ATLAS MOUNTAINS LIE ON TERRACOTTA TILES. THE BAS-RELIEF STONE PIECE IS BY JAN MARTEL. THE *FAUTEUIL* NEAR THE HEARTH DATES FROM THE SEVENTEENTH CENTURY.

BELOW: BASKET-WOVEN MASKS HANG ON A WOODEN COAT-RACK.

RIGHT: JACQUES IS DRAWN TO "MATERIALS THAT ACQUIRE A PATINA"—EARTH, STRAW, WOOD, IRON. HE FOUND THE BASQUE *TORO DE FUEGO* IN PERPIGNAN.

RHAPSODY IN BLUE

If ocher, sienna and umber are intrinsic colors of Provence, so too is blue, in all its various degrees: from the cobalt blue of the Mediterranean to the gray-blue of the Alps; from the violet blue of the lavender fields to the dazzling azure of what Van Gogh called a sky "blanched with heat". For the interior designers Sacha and Lionel Houant it is "the color of life" and it animates their seventeenth-century farmhouse inside and out. Even their cat, Déco, found abandoned in front of their shop in the Lubéron village of Ménerbes, gazes at visitors with eyes that are a startling shade of blue.

But it is not just the use of color that makes their interior landscapes highly original and often dramatic. Entering their private world is like stepping on to a fantastical stage set.

Take, for example, their bedroom, in the middle of which an imposing Napoleon III four-poster bed, draped with a vivid scarlet and white eighteenth-century quilt, holds court. Since the bed seemed "lost", they added an Italian console table, plus a sofa and two chairs upholstered in luxurious crimson velvet. In contrast, a *porte-vête-ments*, for hanging clothes, and two antique church pedestals, converted into bedside tables, were painted a pale blue-gray, and adorned with a pair of *girandole* crystal and gold-wood chandeliers. Even so, the white walls made the room seem "glacial"—so they were brought to life with frescoes, in tones of deep red, honey and pale blue, inspired by scenes from Pompeii. For the floor the Houants chose refurbished terracotta tiles the color of the earth, and the ceiling became the color of the sky, dotted with clouds.

Downstairs, in what was once a granary and is now a salon, the vaulted ceilings and the walls have been painted a blue so intense that it makes you blink: it is the same color as the ceiling of the Provençal chapel where they were married. Here, adding to the sense of fantasy, are a tenderly restored nineteenth-century gondola from a fairground carousel, a miniature *Guignol* theater, and the stone faces of a pair of troubadours resting on the mantelpiece.

The remaining rooms are warmed by Burgundy stone floors and a softer blue, for "the eyes need a rest", but their sense of drama is never entirely absent. Two stone sphinxes guard the entrance to the living room. Between the kitchen and the exquisite entrance hall a fairground horse prances on a silver ball.

*L*EFT: WELCOMING SHADED TERRACES SURROUND THE FARMHOUSE.

BELOW: SACHA'S HOMEMADE *VIN DE NOIX* PROVIDES A WARMING APÉRITIF FOR WINTER NIGHTS. IT IS MADE FROM FRESH WALNUTS, PICKED IN JUNE AT THE FESTIVAL OF ST. JEAN, THEN STEEPED IN RED WINE WITH SUGAR, A VANILLA POD AND A LITTLE EAU DE VIE FOR PRECISELY FIFTY DAYS.

RIGHT: WALLS PATINATED BY THE TRADITIONAL METHOD USING PAINT AND WAX GIVE THE HALLWAY LEADING TO THE FIRST FLOOR A TIMELESS ELEGANCE. THE EIGHTEENTH-CENTURY ITALIAN CONSOLE TABLE AND THE LOUIS XVI TERRACOTTA URN STILL GLORY IN THEIR ORIGINAL PAINT.

𝒜bove: Draped in muslin and a quilt, a magnificent Napoleon III four-poster bed, painted in blue-green and faded gold, stands in Sacha's and Lionel's theatrical bedroom.

Right: Morning sunlight fills the room, emphasizing the dramatic contrast between the crimson velvet upholstery of the nineteenth-century Italian suite and the subtle honey and earth tones of the frescoes. The *porte vêtements* for hanging clothes was made to the Houant's design; on top are two of the late-eighteenth-century boxes (made to store lace caps) that Sacha collects.

CHÂTEAU DE L'ANGE

For as long as she can remember—ever since, as a child, she learnt embroidery from her grandmothers—Edith Mézard has embellished wholly functional things with elements of fantasy. When her own children were born she embroidered their sheets, their pillowcases and, later on, their jeans: "I practically embroidered the children themselves." Even now she cannot resist wielding a needle for at least four or five hours a day to adorn linens, Egyptian cottons and precious cashmeres with intricate monograms and motifs. She is, as she will happily admit, incurably "hooked".

Her lifelong passion for her craft has brought spectacular results. What began as a tiny commercial enterprise called "Lemon Tea, No Sugar" in 1987—when, she felt, her three sons were old enough to need her a little less—now produces two collections a year of exquisitely embroidered household linens in natural shades that sell, under the Edith Mézard label, from New York to Tokyo, from Singapore to Paris. They are handsewn by eleven local women—including Edith, for she counts herself very much a part of the workforce—in an inspirational setting.

The Château de l'Ange in the village of Lumières, named after the stone angel that once hovered on top of the fountain flowing in a garden shaded by chestnut trees, is a proud eighteenth-century house in the heart of the Lubéron, with a rose-pink façade graced with serried ranks of dove-gray shutters. There is a wealth of windows, allowing the house to be suffused with sunlight, and decked with delicate curtains. Many of these have been embroidered by Edith with quotations from some of Provence's most notable sons—Daudet, Pagnol, Giono—testifying to her intoxication with the poetic beauty of their words.

The house's sense of luxury stems from its spaciousness, accentuated by the preponderance of cool beige and white, Edith's favorite colors. But some of the rooms remain a rich ochre, and she has left the original dark red tiles on the floors, to maintain the château's links with its past.

Her workshops and showroom are in the stables, now converted into an airy space where, in July and August each year, she holds three- and four-day embroidery courses. They are run as a kind of "sewing bee" for those who want to learn the secrets of a tradition that is truly ancient, but—now invested with Edith's boundless talent and passion—also freshly contemporary.

*L*EFT: THE OCHER-ROSE FAÇADE OF THE CHÂTEAU DE L'ANGE, BEHIND THE FOUNTAIN WHERE A STONE ANGEL ONCE PERCHED.
TOP: EDITH IN HER KITCHEN, EMBROIDERING MONOGRAMS ON LINEN. THE COMMODIOUS WICKER-BASKET DRAWERS (ABOVE) WERE DESIGNED BY MICHEL BIEHN.

*L*EFT: IN THE SUMMER DINING ROOM A LONG FARMHOUSE TABLE IS SURROUNDED BY GARDEN CHAIRS; WITH ONE STARTLING BLUE EXCEPTION, THE SEAT PADS (HANDMADE BY EDITH) ECHO THE RED TONE OF THE WALLS. THE SHELVES HOLD OLD PROVENÇAL SQUARE FLOWERPOTS AND SMALL POTS FOR CANDLES, FROM HERVÉ BAUME. IN AND UNDER THE WASHBASIN ARE AGED COPPER WATER CONTAINERS.

RIGHT: THE WALLS OF THE HALLWAY ARE PAINTED AN OXBLOOD RED. A PAINTING OF A MADONNA AND CHILD, GIVEN TO EDITH BY A FRIEND, HANGS BETWEEN ANTIQUE CARRIAGE LAMPS FOUND IN L'ISLE-SUR-LA-SORGUE. THE CURVING STAIRCASE IS ORIGINAL TO THE HOUSE, AS ARE THE BANISTER AND THE DARK RED TILES ON THE FLOOR.

*L*EFT: THE FIGURE PRESIDING OVER THE SALON IS DRESSED IN A *COSTUME DE COMTADINE*. BALLS OF PINE CONES ARE BALANCED ON THE TABLE. THE CURTAINS WERE HAND-PRINTED BY ROBERT LE HÉROS.
BELOW: FOUR DECOY BIRDS AND A PIECE OF UNFINISHED ANTIQUE TAPESTRY.
RIGHT: THE SOFA IS COVERED IN NATURAL LINEN. ABOVE IT, A GOLD-PAINTED WOODEN ARROW, FOUND AT MICHEL BIEHN'S, WAS IRRESISTIBLE TO EDITH "BECAUSE ANGELS USE ARROWS TO PIERCE HEARTS".

*T*op and above: Rosemaries add white relief to the predominant greens and grays of box, lauristinus, santolina and sturdy lonicera.

Right: Outside the kitchen Nicole de Vésian added steps to a terrace made of worn stones to create a place where some of her nineteen grandchildren could sit and eat breakfast, in the shade of a fig tree.

Spread across the southern slopes below a medieval Lubéron village, Nicole de Vésian's dramatic garden perfectly reflects the austere beauty of the mountain range it faces. There are no risqué red oleanders, or jarring geraniums—indeed, there are hardly any flowers at all. Rather there is a fragrant abundance of sage and lavender, rosemary and santolina, hardy box and supple yews, gathered from the wild. Yet it is not entirely untamed. Bushes of lavender, sculpted severely into spheres, stand in rows like columns of infantry, and Nicole has cut windows in the foliage to frame the views.

Everywhere there are stones: stone steps, stone walls, stone benches and stones per se; quarried by the process of time and hauled down from the Lubéron, or dredged from the bed of the Durance river. They lie where Nicole has carefully placed them among the plants. Deceptively natural and haphazard, there is nothing random about the design. Nicole was once a consultant for Hermès, and an industrial designer in her own right, and everything in her garden must match her purist aesthetic.

With indomitable vitality, Nicole bought the land and the ruined house that went with it in 1987, when she was in her seventies, and began integrating them so that in color and form they now echo each other, with almost no dividing line between the two. The house is restored, rather than renovated. Its walls are of naked stone or plastered with rough cement. Furniture and furnishings are plain and simple, the colors neutral and subdued. The small wooden armoire in the kitchen was "bought for thruppence" in the village. The curtains were stitched from old linen sheets bought in local markets. The hallway is scattered with smaller stones taken from the riverbed.

There are few paintings on the walls, for Nicole has no need of illusions. Every room she uses looks out over the garden and the incomparable landscape beyond. The summer room she created—where dried flowers on the walls add muted color, and where she spends some of her days restoring old tapestries, simply for the pleasure of it—has a sliding wall made completely of glass.

Tall, slender and graceful as one of her cypresses, Nicole has no more interest in possessions, save one. By creating an extraordinary extension of the Lubéron range, she has become a part of it. Now, she can pretend, all of that strange, magical land belongs to her.

*L*EFT: AN IRON PAN USED FOR *CRÊPES* HANGS ABOVE CENTURY-OLD OLIVE OIL JARS. THE CHURCH BENCH AND CHAIR, LIKE ALMOST EVERY OBJECT THAT NICOLE CARES ABOUT, "COST THRUPPENCE".

RIGHT: COTTON CURTAINS SOLD AT A LO-CAL MARKET BY WEIGHT RATHER THAN DI-MENSION DIFFUSE THE LIGHT THAT BATHES NICOLE'S "SUMMER ROOM", STREAMING THROUGH A FLOOR-TO-CEILING SLIDING GLASS WALL. THIS IS WHERE SHE PLANS HER GARDEN AND FINDS NEW PURPOSES FOR "THINGS THAT LOOK AS IF THEY HAVE LIVED". BEYOND THE FACING WALL, WHERE THISTLES, HOLLYHOCKS AND WHEAT ARE HUNG TO DRY, LIES A SERIES OF AGE-OLD VAULTS. BLUE-GRAY DOORS THAT SHE FOUND ELSEWHERE IN THE HOUSE, AND A SHELF FIXED WITH IRON BRACKETS, FRAME THE ENTRANCE, DIGNIFIED BY PORTRAITS DATING BACK TO 1860. NICOLE'S WORK-TABLE IS A SLAB OF WOOD WITH ROUGH-CUT EDGES, SET ON SIMPLE TRESTLES. IN THE CENTER, FILLED WITH DRIED LAVENDER, IS ONE OF HER LARGE COLLECTION OF OLD BASKETS, WHICH IS RIVALED ONLY BY HER COLLECTION OF HATS.

*A*BOVE: ON ONE OF TWO POT-
TING TABLES MADE OF HANDCARVED STONE,
IN FRONT OF AN OAK TRELLIS SOME 200
YEARS OLD, STANDS A *JARRE D'ANDUZE* THAT
NICOLE HAS BEAUTIFULLY RESTORED.

RIGHT: AN ARRAY OF STONE PROVIDES VER-
NACULAR TEXTURE FOR NICOLE'S UNIQUE
GARDEN: PATCHWORKS OF STONES FROM
THE LUBÉRON MOUNTAINS, WORN BY THE
ELEMENTS; SLABS CARVED BY HAND THREE
CENTURIES AGO AND NOW FASHIONED INTO
FURNITURE; LICHENED STONES SET AMONG
THE BEDS. "BROKEN" CYPRESS SHAPED INTO
COLUMNS AND GIANT SPHERES OF LONICERA
PROVIDE FORM, WHILE WHITE CONVULVULUS
AND BLUE TURCRIUM ADD COLOR.

The passions and certainties that inspire Xavier Nicod are power-ful: a determination to succeed through unremitting work that be-gan when he was in his teens, hungry for knowledge and experi-ence; an almost religious reverence for antiques; not least, a singu-lar vision of Provençal style that is surprisingly ascetic—the an-tithesis of the fussy *faux* fashion he has no time for.

Xavier's vision may be glimpsed at his successful shop in L'Isle-sur-la-Sorgue, which he opened when he was just 24: an Aladdin's Cave overflowing with fantastic and sometimes mysterious *objets d'art* and imposing furniture. But it is most visible at his home: a ruined shell of a 600-year-old three-story village house, uninhabit-ed for a century, which he bought on impulse for twice what he could afford, and spent seven years restoring.

A mustard-colored door opens from the street on to a large room endowed with a vaulted ceiling painted ocher. In an other-wise empty space stands a small washed-blue sideboard between two campaign beds painted a pale gray. Beyond, a small courtyard leads to a walled garden with wild olive trees that have tripled in size since Xavier planted them in 1988, and now shade a rough stone table perfectly positioned for impromptu picnics—if only he had the time.

Winding, well-trodden stone stairs ascend to a huge kitchen with lofty ceilings where almost everything, from the china to the painted cabinets, is ochre or dark red. The floor is made of ancient tiles that he painstakingly collected a few at a time.

In the dining-cum-living room a massive dining table and bat-tered brown leather chairs suggest an English gentleman's club. Similarly uncluttered, his bedroom, reached by climbing up yet more winding stairs, has walls of cool gray-blue, a floor of unvar-nished pine, and a few pieces of magnificently formidable nine-teenth-century furniture. On a small terrace, overlooking medieval rooftops, an antique showerhead is set into the wall, with a shallow zinc tub beneath—for alfresco ablutions.

By now you think you know Xavier's rigorous style, and believe him to be an uncompromising purist. Yet suddenly, as you descend the spiral stairs, your theories are thrown into disarray by a star-tling and intriguing sight: a baby's room painted in gentle colors, with a delicate antique bed dressed in old linen; a silver ball hangs above it, to catch the light and delight a child.

ABOVE: IN THE LIVING ROOM LEATHER ARMCHAIRS AND A CLASSIC CLUB SOFA OF 1930S VINTAGE FORM WHAT XAVIER CALLS 'A GOOD MARRIAGE' WITH A SIMPLE *TABLE DE PÊCHEUR*, DISCOVERED IN A PROVENÇAL FISHERMAN'S CABIN. THE MIRROR IS NINETEENTH CENTURY.

BELOW: DETERMINED NOT TO ALTER THE SIZE OF THE ORIGINAL WINDOW OPENINGS IN THE FAÇADE, XAVIER EVENTUALLY FOUND A GOTHIC WINDOW THAT HE COULD ADAPT TO GIVE A DRAMATIC ASPECT TO A FIRST-FLOOR PASSAGEWAY.

RIGHT: THE EIGHTEENTH-CENTURY WALL TILES BEHIND THE COUNTER TOPS IN THE KITCHEN WERE USED TO LINE THE INSIDE OF WINE VATS AND ARE HARD TO FIND IN SUCH PRISTINE CONDITION. THE CUPBOARD DOORS ARE MADE OF CAST IRON; THE SINK OF MARBLE NINE INCHES THICK AND SO HEAVY THAT IT TOOK SIX OF XAVIER'S FRIENDS TO CARRY IT UP THE STAIRS. HE LIKES TO IMAGINE THAT THE WOODEN HORSE WAS CARVED BY A GRANDFATHER FOR HIS GRANDSON IN THE NINETEENTH CENTURY. THE OAK DINING TABLE AND CHAIRS DATE FROM THE SAME ERA.

*L*EFT: MUSIC SHEETS LINE THE WALLS OF THE CHILD'S BEDROOM. THE BED IS NINETEENTH CENTURY, THE LAMP MOROCCAN. SILVER BALLS LIKE THOSE HANGING FROM THE CEILING WERE USED IN GRAND CHÂTEAUX TO ATTRACT BIRDS.

ABOVE: THE RUSH-SEATED *RADASSIÉ* AT THE FOOT OF XAVIER'S BED IS PROVENÇAL. THE IRON SCULPTURES ARE CONTEMPORARY.

RIGHT: IN THE GLASS-FRONTED BATHROOM LEAF-SHAPED CANDLE HOLDERS "GROW" ON A TURN-OF-THE-CENTURY TRELLIS SCREEN. THE IRON STORK CARRIES SOAP. MODERN FLOOR TILES ADD SPLASHES OF COLOR.

LACROIX RETURNS TO ARLES

Of all the enduring memories of his childhood in Arles, the most evocative for Christian Lacroix are of an intimate hotel on the Place du Forum, where the rich peasant sensuousness of Provence—the inspiration for his vibrant designs—encountered the fashionable *beau monde* of the time. Run by the wonderfully eccentric Germaine Bessières, a former cabaret dancer with a taste for outrageous costumes, the Grand Hôtel Nord-Pinus was a favorite haunt of the likes of Hemingway, Picasso and Jean Cocteau, and, most of all, of the proud, snake-hipped matadors of the *corrida*. It was from the balcony of the hotel's suite number 10 that the great *Dominguin*, dressed in white and gold and splashed with crimson from the wounds of his most epic conquest, received the plaudits of the crowd—in much the same way as couturier Lacroix is now showered with praise and flowers by his adoring fans.

By the time the young Christian left Provence for Paris in 1973 the Nord-Pinus had lost what Cocteau had called its "soul", and there were no longer extravagant parties or card games lasting until dawn. Germaine still rose from her seaweed bath in the early afternoon to take her place in the sun on a bench by the hotel's front door, but there were no more guests to welcome. With the roof ruined, and the building slipping into decay, she made a small apartment in the reception area and, attended only by a *valet de jour* and a *valet de nuit*, waited out her days.

So Christian was overjoyed when, in 1987—after the triumphant debut of the first House of Lacroix collection—he returned to Arles and discovered that Germaine had sold the Nord-Pinus to Anne Igou, a young Provençale from the Camargue who was determined to restore the hotel to its former glory. Walking in to introduce himself to Anne, he offered to help her in any way he could, and soon became her most tireless supporter. When the hotel reopened, after eighteen months of careful restoration, Christian staged a fashion show, bringing back to Arles the peacock colors, borrowed from Provence, that he has made his hallmark: the scarlet of poppies, the vivid golden-yellow of sunflowers, the sumptuous purple of grapes, the black of Cocteau's long sweeping cape.

Now the matadors and the nights of glamor have returned to the Nord-Pinus, and for Christian—and, he says, "for all Arlesians" —the spirit of the great *Dominguin* lives on once more.

*L*EFT: PHOTOGRAPHS ON THE WALL BEHIND THE BAR AT THE GRAND HÔTEL NORD-PINUS, AND COSTUMES IN A GLASS CASE, PAY TRIBUTE TO BULLFIGHTERS, WHO INSPIRED THE CHANGING CUBICLE—CROWNED WITH A TOREADOR'S HAT—IN CHRISTIAN LACROIX'S ARLES BOUTIQUE (TOP). ABOVE: A PICTURE OF THE DESIGNER ALSO HANGS IN THE HOTEL'S BAR.

*A*BOVE: Nestling in tall grass, a picnic basket with food, wine and flower-printed Souleiado fabric evokes an impromptu outdoor lunch on the starkly beautiful Camargue plains. RIGHT: A Souleiado homage to the Camargue cult of the bull. A table on the ranch of Annie and Henri Laurent, close friends of the Demérys, is laid with a Souleiado tablecloth and tableware decorated with bull and horse motifs.

THE HEART OF SOULEIADO

Fourteen miles south of Avignon, where the width of the Rhône river is all that separates the historic towns of Tarascon and Beaucaire, there is an elegant seventeenth-century townhouse that stands as a fitting memorial to the man who, almost single-handed, rescued an ancient craft that was in danger of dying out and turned it into a thriving industry. It was around the time the house was built that traders from the Levant first brought exuberantly colored block-printed fabrics to Provence from India. These *indiennes*, as they were called, proved so popular that they were soon made locally, particularly in Tarascon, and quickly decimated the French silk and wool industries, causing Louis XIV to ban them—a prohibition that only made them all the more coveted. But by 1933, when Charles Deméry took over one of Tarascon's last remaining fabric works from his uncle, it was making only scarves for women working in the fields, and the tradition of *indiennes* had virtually vanished. He renamed the company Souleiado, which in Provençal means, as close as it can be translated, "the sun's rays shining through a cloud after the rain", and set out on a crusade to spread what is now one of the most distinctive notions of Provence around the world.

M. Deméry made his fabrics in the way they had been made for centuries—tightly woven by hand, then painted with vegetable dyes, each detail of the intricate patterns applied layer by layer from blocks of fruitwood carved with masterly skill—but to sometimes sombre monochromes he added vivacious new colors and a whole range of fashions and styles. Slowly the business grew, until the brilliant sun-kissed prints from Tarascon were seen everywhere: in the Lincoln Room of the Kennedy White House; on the shelves of Fifth Avenue department stores; providing the favorite faded shirts of Pablo Picasso and the dresses of Jeanne Moreau; incorporated into the vibrant fashions of Christian Lacroix.

By the time M. Deméry died in 1986 production methods had been thoroughly modernized, but the tradition he did so much to preserve lives on. For the Tarascon headquarters of Souleiado—which, run by his three children, continues as a family dynasty—contains in the spacious attics that were once the workshops a craft museum that holds among its treasures a legacy of priceless antique fabrics, and 40,000 of the printing blocks that made them so.

*B*ELOW: CHARLES DEMÉRY'S
SUCCESSORS FIND INSPIRATION IN AN
ARCHIVE THAT PRESERVES AND CLASSIFIES
40,000 COPPER-LAMINATED FRUITWOOD
PRINTING BLOCKS.

RIGHT: THE OLDEST BLOCKS IN THE
ARCHIVES DATE FROM THE EIGHTEENTH CEN-
TURY, WHEN FABRICS CALLED *INDIENNES*
WERE ALL THE RAGE. PRINTERS MIXED SE-
CRET COMBINATIONS OF NATURAL DYES DE-
RIVED FROM PLANTS AND EARTH FROM
ROUSSILLON (ABOVE) IN COPPER PANS
(ABOVE LEFT) THEN COLORED THE BLOCKS
AND APPLIED THEM TO THE FABRICS.

SKILL IN QUILT-MAKING WAS AT
ONE TIME CONSIDERED A NECESSARY AT-
TRIBUTE FOR A YOUNG WOMAN HOPING TO
ATTRACT THE ATTENTION OF A MARRIAGE-
ABLE MAN. THE QUILTWORK (LEFT, BELOW
AND RIGHT) IS PADDED WITH COTTON TO
PROVIDE WARMTH DURING VISITS OF THE
MISTRAL. THE HEIRS TO CHARLES DEMÉRY'S
ENTERPRISE DRAW INSPIRATION FROM AN IM-
MENSE PATRIMONY OF PROVENÇAL ARTISTRY.

A Passion for Ceramics

Just as Sanary is a sleepy fishing village left largely untouched by the annual tourist invasion of Provence, so there are weekly *brocante* markets along the coast that remain unspoiled; where prices are reasonable, and where at least some of the stallholders are not dealers but people who have emptied their attics. In the markets of La Seyne, Le Lavandou and Hyères—to name just three—there are still treasures to be found, and each weekend the two partners who form LuluBerlu set off early on a never-ending quest to find the basic raw material for their ingenious enterprise: plates.

Natacha Nokin ("Lulu"), a former fashion stylist from Brussels with incurable wanderlust, and Charlie Degrelle ("Berlu"), a dancer and model from Paris, who came south for a week and never returned, have an insatiable appetite for old Provençal porcelain. In the garage of their home-cum-workshop-cum-showroom in Sanary there are stored, at any one time, some 5,000 plates, categorized first by how the pattern was applied—*au pochoir* (transfer), *sérigraphie* (screen printed), and, the most valuable, handpainted—and then by color.

Every working day they methodically break them - or rather, cut them up into precise pieces with tiler's pliers of the sort in use since Roman times, in order to create eye-catchingly original mosaics. Devising their patterns as they proceed, piece by piece, they transform furniture and objects—"treasures" often found in the same *brocante* markets as the plates—into fantastical works of art that are also functional: vases, dressing tables, shelves, chests, cabinets, mirrors, bird houses, backgammon boards and even billiard tables.

Now they aspire to greater things. Their original inspiration came from the Spanish architect Antoni Gaudí, and they have made the pilgrimage to Barcelona to view his dazzling legacy—have marveled, for example, at his phantasmagorical mosaics on the façade and roof of the Casa Batlló. Like Gaudí, they want to decorate whole buildings with kaleidoscopes of intricate patterns and colors, though using old porcelain rather than tiles, and in a style that is very much their own. The problem is, the supply of old plates is finite, even in the attics and unspoiled markets of Provence. Fortunately, Natacha still travels, always seeking the sun, and Portugal—she has discovered—is amply supplied with plates.

*L*EFT: CUSHIONS THAT NATACHA MADE RECLINE ON AN ANTIQUE TEAK SOFA FROM THAILAND.

ABOVE: WITH ITS COLUMNS AND WROUGHT-IRON RAILINGS, THE FAÇADE OF THE VILLA HAS A COLONIAL FEEL.

BELOW: A LULUBERLU TABLE OF BLUE AND GREEN MOSAIC.

*L*EFT: BACKGAMMON IS EX-
TREMELY POPULAR IN THE MIDI *À L'HEURE
DE L'APÉRITIF*; THIS BACKGAMMON TABLE IS
LULUBERLU'S MOST SUCCESSFUL DESIGN.
ITS ROUNDED CORNERS AND SEMICIRCLE
MOTIF ARE MADE USING PLATES.

BELOW: A SMALL PART OF NATACHA'S
ECLECTIC COLLECTION OF FURNITURE AND
OBJECTS PICKED UP ON HER TRAVELS.

RIGHT: IN THE KITCHEN A METAL BASE
FOUND IN A FLEA MARKET HOLDS A HARVEST
OF VEGETABLES. A SMALL TERRACOTTA
BOWL FROM PORTUGAL WAS GIVEN A SIMPLE
YELLOW AND GREEN DESIGN WITH A BRUSH.

*A*BOVE LEFT: THE CONSOLE
TABLE AND MIRROR TOOK THE LULUBERLU
PARTNERS SIX MONTHS TO COMPLETE; COL-
LECTING HANDPAINTED PLATES FOR THE
CONSOLE'S INTRICATE FLOWER DESIGN
(ABOVE) WAS A PAINSTAKING BUSINESS.
BELOW: THE MOSAIC PLANT POT ON THE
DINING-ROOM *DESSERTE* WAS MADE WITH
PLATES DECORATED *AU POCHOIR*.
RIGHT: CERAMICS FROM VALLAURIS IS ON
DISPLAY IN ONE OF THE BEDROOMS, UNDER A
COLLECTION OF OLD CÔTE D'AZUR SOU-
VENIR PHOTOGRAPHS.

OBJECTS OF DESIRE

In the main street of L'Isle-sur-la-Sorgue, in a satisfyingly symmetrical nineteenth-century townhouse with rooms as high as they are wide, a hallway leads to a small room where there is an atmosphere of Provençal tradition so evocative that you can almost smell it. It has the faint aroma of camphor and lavender that comes from the uppermost shelves of linen cupboards; or from trunks packed long ago and not since disturbed.

Michel Biehn is both a scholar of and dealer in antique textiles, and a passionate conservationist of what he says they represent: "the patrimony" of Provence. It was not his first choice of vocation, nor was Provence where he always chose to live: he has been, chameleon-like, a journalist in Athens, a hatmaker in London, a florist in Venice, and a theatre lighting designer in the former Yugoslavia. He is, however, a son of the south, brought up in what was once the provincial capital, Arles, and he was drawn back by his roots. In Aix-en-Provence he met Catherine, the woman who would become his wife, and finally accepted that his days of restless, distant travel were over.

It was in flea markets closer to home that together they discovered neglected treasures, for antique Provençal textiles were not highly regarded or valued in the early 1980s. They both became enthralled by the extraordinary techniques; by colors sometimes vivid and naïve, sometimes as subtle as the hues of the Lubéron landscape; by patterns carved by artisans on wooden blocks a quarter of a millennium ago.

In 1987 Michel's definitive history of Provençal textiles was published, and they opened their own antique textile shop in Aix. Then they discovered L'Isle-sur-la-Sorgue—made into a miniature Venice by its multiple canals—and, eventually, the house that is now both their home and their shop. They sell antique furniture and objects, as well as fabrics, and contemporary pieces made to Michel's designs. As if all this were not enough, having produced a cookery book that introduced his grandmother's recipes to Britain and America as well as France, every day Michel cooks, for family, friends and staff. In an immense space, encompassing four stories, with only the attic reserved as a magical playroom for the Biehns' two children, it is difficult to tell where "the shop" begins or ends, or which of those who fill it are customers, and which are friends. Frequently they are both.

*L*EFT: A NATURAL PINE ARMOIRE HOLDS EIGHTEENTH- AND NINETEENTH-CENTURY HANDBLOCKED QUILTS, PART OF THE PATRIMONY OF PROVENCE THAT MICHEL BIEHN IS PASSIONATE TO CONSERVE. THE CHAIR IS NINETEENTH-CENTURY FRENCH OAK, MADE "IN THE TASTE OF THE RENAISSANCE" AND COVERED WITH HANDWOVEN RAW SILK. ON THE TABLE THE NINETEENTH-CENTURY TIAN BOWL MADE OF OCHRE-YELLOW CLAY WAS USED FOR SOAKING FRUIT IN SUGAR TO MAKE CANDIED SWEETS, A LOCAL SPECIALITY.

ABOVE: MICHEL ON THE STEPS OF THE SHOP THAT IS ALSO HIS HOME, WITH HIS BULLDOGS, DENTELLE AND DAVIDOFF.

*L*EFT: FOR THE BIEHNS' EVER-
BUSY KITCHEN, WITH ITS ORIGINAL TERRAZZO
FLOOR, MICHEL DESIGNED BASKETWEAVE
CHAIRS AND A TABLE MADE FROM A SLAB OF
LAVA ROCK, SET ON AN IRON FRAME. THE
DRESSER IS NINETEENTH CENTURY.

BELOW: THE PATCHWORK CURTAINS BEHIND
THE *LIT DE REPOS* WERE EMBROIDERED IN
THE LAST CENTURY BY FRENCH NUNS.

RIGHT: TERRACOTTA BIRDS PAINTED BY PAUL
FOUQUE IN THE 1940S PERCH ON AN OLD
AQUARIUM FILLED WITH SEASHELLS. THE
TABLE IS ONE OF SEVERAL PIECES OF FURNI-
TURE MADE FROM DRIFTWOOD GATHERED IN
THE CAMARGUE.

In winter, when most of the farmers' markets in Provence are hibernating, Brigitte Delebecque carries out her research. Combing secondhand bookshops in Aix and Arles, and libraries and flea markets, and the bookshelves of indulgent friends, she hunts for long-forgotten recipes for gastronomic delights that she will make at home then sell around the world.

In January she can be found in Maussane, buying the first pressings of the finest olive oil; or in Richerenches, in the enclave of Valréas, where the truffle is venerated at a pungent mass held each year in the abbey, and where she buys her supplies from the families who have been bringing their treasures here for generations.

Spring reawakens the produce markets, and brings the first new vegetables, and shopping consumes her days. Each trip to the market takes a whole morning, for she goes without a list and with an entirely open mind, stopping at every stall, looking for surprises. These are often to be found at *le petit marché* held each Saturday morning in Vaison-la-Romaine, where the stallholders bring produce from their own gardens. In early summer the first fruit arrives: melons from Cavaillon, then cherries and apricots from Vaison. In autumn, there are apples and pears from Lagnes.

And all the while, in her kitchen at home, using the recipes she has diligently gleaned, Brigitte cooks and boils and stirs and mixes: fruits and red onions for sensuous confitures; almonds and anchovies blended into savory pommades; oils perfumed with basil and aniseed; aubergines, red peppers and tomatoes that become conserves with wonderfully exotic names such as *"L'aubergine amoureuse des épices"*, *"Les poivrons doux mais capricieux"*, and *"Les tomates fascinées par les herbes"*.

Her most precious recipes are the ones that are "old, old, old"—bequeathed by herbalists and grandmothers who knew how to marry the "healthful pleasures and virtues of plants" with sinful alcohol, and store it in jars to be turned in the sun for precisely forty days, yielding "a selfish mixture to be drunk stealthily, in very small quantities".

There are elixirs for almost every occasion: "for the anxious hours" (vanilla, orange flowers, spices); "for euphoria rediscovered" (oranges, lemons, honey); "for awaiting your beloved" (citronella and syrup); and, tantalizingly, "elixir of mad, passionate love". The ingredients of that are secret.

*R*IGHT: A *TABLE D'ABONDANCE* ARRANGED IN THE GARDEN OF AN EIGHTEENTH-CENTURY HOUSE IN MALAUCÈNE SHOWS SOME OF BRIGITTE'S PRODUCTS (SUCH AS "PINK PREFERENCE" AND "MASCULINE CERTITUDE"), AND THE FRESH SEASONAL INGREDIENTS FROM WHICH THEY ARE MADE. FOR HER *"COLÈRE PROVENÇALE"* RED PEPPERS, GARLIC, TOMATOES AND OLIVE OIL WILL MAKE A MAGICAL MIXTURE.

ABOVE: THE HOUSE PLAYING HOST TO BRIGITTE'S CREATIONS WAS BUILT FOR THE MARQUIS DES ISNARDS AND HIS WIFE, WHO ARE DEPICTED ON THE FOUNTAIN HEADS.

*T*OP: *FLACONS* CONTAINING SUG-
AR-CANE VINEGAR FLAVORED USING WILD
VIOLET PETALS.

ABOVE: AN ASSORTMENT OF BRIGITTE'S
ELIXIRS AND JAMS.

RIGHT: A WATERMELON JAM *TARTINE*, SUN-
LIGHT AND SHADE, AND BRIGITTE'S NINE-
TEENTH-CENTURY WROUGHT-IRON BED FORM
A SIESTA FANTASY.

*A*BOVE: MANY ROOMS IN
MARIE-STELLA'S HOME ARE ON SEPARATE
LEVELS, AND STAIRCASES ABOUND. THIS ONE
COMBINES HANDMADE MEXICAN TILES AND
TERRACOTTA TREADS WHOSE WARM EARTHY
COLORS ALSO ADORN THE WALL AND COUN-
TERS OF THE MUCH-USED KITCHEN (RIGHT).
HERE, DIFFUSED LIGHT FROM A CHURCH-IN-
SPIRED STAINED-GLASS WINDOW CARESSES A
PROVENÇAL SIDEBOARD MADE FROM WAL-
NUT. THE CROCKERY IS MOSTLY FROM
GLOBE TROTTER, ALTHOUGH MARIE-STELLA
HAS ACQUIRED SOME PIECES THROUGH
COUPS DE CŒUR IN ANTIQUES SHOPS.

The diversity of styles that marks Provence is often the result of "invasion" by outsiders who bring with them concepts and inspirations that are assimilated and thus enrich the local culture. Sometimes the best new ideas are actively imported.

Marie-Stella Castanier, an interior decorator from Avignon, had just turned 40 when she went to New York to visit her daughter, and was seduced by America. She stayed for a year, traveling around the country and down into Mexico, absorbing a very different southern style from that of her native Midi. It was only when she discovered Santa Fé, and announced she might live there permanently, that her daughter insisted it was time for her to go home.

But the experience changed her life irrevocably, for it imbued her with a design concept that borrowed from those influences yet was uniquely her own. Back home in Avignon, she began by importing furniture from the United States. Now it is made by local artisans in Provence while her company—appropriately called Globe Trotter—imports objects, made to her design, from all over the world: tiles from Mexico, wrought iron from Poland, pottery from Portugal and Italy, and ceramics from Vietnam. She sells her collection from two shops in Avignon and Paris, and through department stores throughout Europe—and, ironically, the United States.

She travels constantly and seems endlessly creative, bringing out fresh lines "whenever I have a new idea, which is often". The influences on her are obviously now global but firmly anchored by what she regards as the essential ethos of Provence: her designs, like the spirit of her native land, are simple, unpretentious, generous and authentic. It is the very lack of sophistication, and her sensitivity to rough textures and the colors of the countryside, that make her work so appealing.

Though she remains infatuated with New York, she is no longer a "city girl". She now lives "the perfect life" in a small village near Avignon, where the three *lavoirs* are still in daily use. Her home, which serendipitously she saw advertised in an estate agent's window, is a barn, part of the outbuildings of a château. She restored it from scratch, and now it is filled with the objects she sells in her shops, while her shops are re-creations of her house. Hers is a highly personal style, which succeeds because it is decidedly not about "style" at all.

*L*EFT: IN A CORNER OF THE SA-
LON A GILT-FRAMED ANTIQUE MIRROR RE-
FLECTS AN OLD CUPBOARD DOOR—PATINAT-
ED *À L'ANCIENNE*—THAT CONCEALS A TELE-
VISION. THE ELEGANT ROUND TABLE IN THE
FOREGROUND—A *GUÉRIDON*—CONTRASTS
WITH A HOMESPUN WOODEN CHAIR FOUND
IN A FLEA MARKET.

ABOVE: MARIE-STELLA DECIDED TO BUY THE
HOUSE THE MOMENT SHE SAW THE STONE
FOUNTAIN IN THE GARDEN.

RIGHT: A CONTEMPORARY FOUR-POSTER
BED, AND A SOLID PINE BUREAU FROM
GLOBE TROTTER FURNISH THE GUEST BED-
ROOM. THE CUPBOARD DOORS WERE MADE
BY A LOCAL CARPENTER. THE BEDLINEN IS A
FAMILY HEIRLOOM.

*L*EFT: A DOOR MADE OF GLASS AND STRIPPED ANTIQUE PINE OPENS TO REVEAL THE GUEST BATHROOM, WHERE STONES FROM THE DURANCE RIVER HAVE BEEN SET IN A RUSTIC CEMENT WALL.

ABOVE: THE SAME TECHNIQUE HAS BEEN APPLIED TO THE DINING-ROOM TABLE'S CEMENT TOP, WHICH MATCHES A PROFUSION OF THE BRIGHT YELLOW MIMOSA SO CHARACTERISTIC OF THE REGION.

BELOW: THE IDENTICAL TWIN OF THE FLEA-MARKET CHAIR IN THE SALON CURRENTLY RESIDES IN MARIE-STELLA'S BEDROOM, WHERE THE REST OF THE FURNITURE IS OF GLOBE TROTTER DESIGN. THE ANGEL AND PICTURES WERE FOUND IN *BROCANTES*, THE BEDDING AND COVERS ARE BY RALPH LAUREN, AND THE WALLS WERE PAINTED VANILLA USING NATURAL PIGMENTS FROM THE LUBÉRON.

*A*BOVE: IN THE SUMMER MICHEL AND JOEL OFTEN EAT OUTDOORS, SURROUNDED BY GERANIUMS AND AGAPANTHUS. FOR MORE FORMAL FEASTS THEY USE THE SUMMER DINING ROOM, WITH ITS CHANDELIER BOUGHT FROM A CHARITY SHOP.
RIGHT: THE WINTER DINING ROOM CONTAINS A RESTORATION CHAIR FROM ARLES (IN THE FOREGROUND), A KILIM RUG, MIRRORS WITH SHELL FRAMES, BISTRO TABLES, A LOUIS XVI SOFA AND A CHAIR (LEFT) THAT IS ALSO LOUIS XVI BUT TYPICALLY PROVENÇAL BECAUSE OF ITS SIZE AND RUSH-BOTTOMED SEAT.

Given that there are now few houses for sale in Provence that have not been at least partially "restored", it was unlikely that Michel Klein would easily find what he was looking for. As the most outstanding prodigy of the new generation of leading French fashion designers, who showed his first sketches to the house of Yves Saint Laurent when he was just 15, his sense of style is too individual and ingrained to adapt to other people's foibles. So with his companion, Joel Fournier, he rejected some sixty houses before arriving, one summer evening, at a humble sixteenth-century farmhouse in the Alpilles, only part of which was for sale, and deciding immediately it was for them. Friends thought them quite mad.

Not any more. Through the gradual acquisition of adjoining parts of the building, their home is now much bigger than it was, but remains supremely unpretentious. Yet there is a symmetry and richness of detail in the decor that is positively breathtaking.

Michel's distinctive genius as a designer lies in his ability to create elegance with a twist. Just as his clothes are classically beautiful, yet at the same time easy to wear, so the house is exquisitely decorated, yet wonderfully comfortable, and frequently full of friends, children and animals. There are no obvious rules to the design— but gradually you notice that the blue in a yellow and blue striped cover of an armchair perfectly picks up the blue of a time-worn rug, which in turn echoes the pattern of a nearby stool, and so on, to create a kind of interlocking jigsaw. In his world things are not meant to match, except in terms of sensibility. Patterns mix with solid colors, while furniture and objects are a fusion of styles and eras: pieces from exotic parts of the world are grouped in "families" with works by modern designers such as Tom Dixon and Öm Gudmundarson, placed next to venerable antiques or curiosities found in flea markets.

Above all, there is his extraordinary use of vivid colors—extraordinary for a couturier renowned for his adherence to navy, cream and, above all, black. Liberated from the constraints of fashion, and inspired by the legendary southern light, Michel has painted each room a warm ocher yellow, or rich cardinal red, or lavender, or green, or, in the case of the kitchen, blue and white speckles like a bird's egg. What was once an ordinary house now literally glows with his artistry.

*L*EFT: IN THE SALON EXOTIC OBJECTS SURROUND A NAPOLEON III SOFA: GREEN-PAINTED FUNERARY STATUES FROM SUMATRA; TWO WOODEN OARS FROM PERSIA; TWO *BAIGNOIRES* (MINIATURE BATH TUBS) IN MURANO GLASS; TWO AFRICAN OS-TRICH EGGS THAT LOOK LIKE FLASKS; UNDER THE TABLES, BASKETS FROM BALI AND SEASHELLS FROM MADAGASCAR. THE PAINT-INGS OF STAR CONSTELLATIONS WERE DONE BY JOEL'S NEPHEW, OLIVIER VENARD.

ABOVE: AT ANOTHER END OF THE SALON TWO LOW CHAIRS OF BLACKENED PEARWOOD AND A TABLE WITH TWISTED FEET ARE ALSO NAPOLEON III.

*A*BOVE: THE DIMINUTIVE LARDER ON THE KITCHEN COUNTER TOP IS AN EIGHTEENTH-CENTURY *GARDE-MANGER*. THE FAIENCES ON THE WALL ARE ALSO EIGHTEENTH-CENTURY.

BELOW: MORE FAÏENCE WARE—CHINESE, JAPANESE AND FRENCH—IS DISPLAYED ON A BATIK-COVERED ROUND TABLE IN A SMALL DINING ROOM.

RIGHT: AFTER LIVING WITH WHITE WALLS FOR FIVE YEARS, MICHEL AND JOEL WOKE UP ONE MORNING AND DECIDED TO PAINT. THEY MIXED LOCAL PIGMENTS, PLASTER AND ACRYLIC COLOR IN BIG BOWLS, THEN SET TO WORK. IN THE KITCHEN THEY WIPED OFF PAINT WITH A DAMP RAG, CREATING A SPECKLED-EGG EFFECT. THE "MARQUEE STRIPES" ON THE CEILING WERE PAINTED BY THEIR FRIEND VINCENT SCALLI. IN THE KITCHEN WHAT LOOKS LIKE A STOVE IS A RARE *MURISSOIR DE VER À SOIE*, USED TWO CENTURIES AGO TO DRY SILK COCOONS. ON THE WALL IS A GRAIN MERCHANT'S DISPLAY BOARD FROM THE NINETEENTH CENTURY, SHOWING SAMPLES OF VEGETABLE SEEDS.

Left: In the "blue bedroom" a Louis XVI bed is covered with mattress ticking. The two blackened pearwood chairs are Napoleon III, upholstered in Rubelli fabric.

Below: The "red bedroom" dazzles with a Provençal quilt on a Louis XVI bed.

Right: The modern wrought-iron bed in the "green bedroom" was inspired by Louis XVI style. The bookcase cupboard came from a charity shop and was painted by Joel "in about one hour".

Exuberant
Creativity

*T*his
magical land never ceases to entice and beguile

fresh suitors. Their eclectic creativity,

reflected in a wide diversity of visions, heralds

the inspiring spirit of a new ethos.

*T*op and above: In its days as a working farm poultry ranged free in the sun-dappled *basse-cour*. Now it is filled with the scents of rosemary and lavender, and the aromas of cooking. Right: Old carved stones found at Chanteduc, suggesting it is the site of a Roman ruin, make perfect platforms for scented geraniums by the kitchen window.

FARMHOUSE SIMPLICITY

In a 200-year-old farmhouse named Chanteduc, set amid fertile vineyards and orchards, Patricia and Walter Wells devote themselves to "perfecting paradise"—by making it serenely simple.

In an ancient bread oven, set into the wall of a sun-dappled courtyard, a *gigot d'agneau* roasts slowly, the juices dripping into a potato gratin below. In the kitchen, which looks out on to banks of iris and lavender, fava beans from the garden are cooking on the Cornue stove. On the table is a bowl of salad leaves sprinkled with bright yellow flowers plucked from a broom bush that taste as delicious as they look. The wine comes from grapes that grow prolifically on the couple's own vines.

The kitchen is flooded with light even on a dull day, a place where friends can gather to watch Patricia cook or, better still, to help. The walls are painted a creamy-beige; the cabinets are the color of buttermilk; the tiles that cover every surface are a deeper buttercup yellow. Sun-baked pots and jars and dishes, delved for in flea markets, in glorious greens and vivid ocher, jostle amicably with creamy-yellow Provençal china handmade by craftsmen in Apt. There is an old dark green cheese larder, now a decorator's fad, which Patricia genuinely uses for cheese. A copper kettle whistles on the cooker.

And all along one wall, stacked from floor to ceiling, are handmade shelves crammed with cookery books, including the *Food Lover's Guides to Paris* and *France* that have helped make Patricia the most influential restaurant critic and food writer in France—no small accomplishment for an American from Milwaukee who arrived in Paris in 1980, speaking "not one word" of French and knowing "next to nothing" about French cuisine.

Few have done more to celebrate and preserve the French tradition of simple, unfussy cooking. She has crisscrossed the country, travelling 30,000 miles, seeking out, as she puts it, "goat farmers, cheesemakers, fishermen, certifiably insane bakers, *escargot* processors, sea-salt rakers, walnut oil pressers, winemakers, pig wholesalers, and two brothers who make a living growing courgette blossoms": people fiercely proud of their crafts, and in some danger of extinction. Once back in Chanteduc, Patricia assembles their foods and their recipes and marries them to produce a cuisine that is in tune with the new spirit of the age: dishes that are a joy to prepare and cook—as well as to eat.

*A*BOVE: THE WEST-FACING
"CHAMPAGNE TERRACE" WAS DESIGNED FOR
WATCHING THE SPECTACULAR SUNSETS AT
CHANTEDUC, UNTIL PATRICIA AND WALTER
DISCOVERED THAT UNDER THE BRANCHES OF
THE HUGE UMBRELLA PINE A "MICROCLI-
MATE" PROVIDES COOL BREEZES ON EVEN
THE HOTTEST SUMMER DAYS. NOW THE TER-
RACE IS USED ALL DAY LONG, FROM BREAK-
FAST TO SUNSET DINNER.

RIGHT: LAVENDER OUTSIDE A GUESTROOM
LOAD THE AIR WITH A SCENT PATRICIA
ADORES—AND YIELD ONE OF THE INGREDI-
ENTS FOR HER LAVENDER HONEY ICE CREAM.

*L*EFT: IN A KITCHEN BATHED
WITH SOFT LIGHT, WHICH IT BOTH ABSORBS
AND REFLECTS, PATRICIA BAKES BREAD EACH
MORNING: "THEN I FEEL I HAVE ACCOM-
PLISHED SOMETHING."
ABOVE: HER SOURDOUGH WITH FLAX, SUN-
FLOWER AND SESAME SEEDS WAITS TO RISE.
TOP: CLOS CHANTEDUC, TRULY THE HOUSE
WINE, IS MADE ORGANICALLY FROM THREE
VARIETIES OF GRAPE.

*L*EFT: THE GUEST ROOM, ONCE THE *PIGEONNIER*, OFFERS THE LUXURY OF PRIVACY BECAUSE IT IS SEPARATE FROM THE REST OF THE HOUSE. THE BEDS, WITH THEIR CHINESE-STYLE BRASS BEDHEADS, AND THE PINE CHEST, WERE FOUND IN LOCAL MARKETS. ON EITHER SIDE OF A PHOTOGRAPH THAT PATRICIA TOOK WHILE RESEARCHING *THE FOOD LOVER'S GUIDE TO FRANCE* ARE TWO OF HUSBAND WALTER'S COLLECTION OF "AT LEAST FIFTY" STRAW HATS.

RIGHT: THEIR BEDROOM, LOOKING OUT OVER CHANTEDUC'S VINEYARDS, AND WITH A BREATHTAKING VIEW OF MONT VENTOUX, CAPTURES THE MORNING LIGHT. THE BRASS BED, BOUGHT LOCALLY, IS DRESSED WITH ANTIQUE LINENS AND QUILTS THAT PATRICIA HAS COLLECTED OVER THE YEARS, AND THAT SHE CHANGES TO REFLECT THE MOOD OF THE SEASONS. THE BOOKSHELVES WERE PAINTED TO MATCH THE HUE OF THE UNDERSIDE OF AN OLIVE LEAF.

OUT OF AFRICA

Built with due deference to the *mistral*, which can sweep ferociously down the Rhône valley from Siberia, the mid-nineteenth-century farmhouse painstakingly restored by Sarah St. George looks, from the outside, typically Provençal: square, solid and soberly practical. Only the vivid lime-green shutters hint at what awaits inside the thick stone walls and sensibly sized windows. Even Sarah—a barrister-turned-banker-turned-writer—seems surprised by the "fantasy of color" created by her friend Maxime de la Falaise, a fashion and furniture designer. "One would never have a house that looked like this anywhere else in the world," says Sarah.

A spacious entrance hall, where soft pink walls harmonize with the pale pistachio and darker greens of the floor tiles and furniture, is designed, she jokes, to lull the visitor into "a false sense of calm". Certainly it does not prepare you for the spectacle of the living room, a converted barn, where only the stone floor and an antique chimneypiece remain unpainted by Maxime. Broad stripes of cadmium yellow and red ochre cover the walls, while the window embrasures are pale blue. The ceiling beams are painted in dense abstract patterns influenced by African and pygmy art, which Maxime sees as being "somewhere between language and décor". Even the radiators are painted in African stripes. The furniture fabrics are an eclectic mixture of damson, yellow, blue, green and orange.

Maxime's African theme returns in the dining room, where an antique armoire is colored entirely in zigzags of red, black, cerulean blue and yellow. The walls are washed in stripes of sea-green and sea-blue, and so too is the ceiling. Placed so that the cook can be with her guests, a deep-jade Aga cooker sits against a wall on which Maxime has created an extravagant mosaic of gravel and Venetian glass. The main kitchen beyond has yellow walls and cupboards painted the brilliant blue of the Aegean.

Upstairs the walls and ceilings of the principal bedrooms, and of the four guest rooms, are washed in calmer hues: pale blues and greens, lilac and French gray. But there is hardly a surface that has not been touched by Maxime's paintbrush, and her extraordinary imagination. In Sarah's bathroom, above a handbasin painted to look like marble, a wooden cabinet encasing a mirror is adorned with "lucky tortoises" to "cheer me up in the mornings".

*L*EFT: IN THE DINING ROOM A TURKISH OIL LANTERN HANGS ABOVE A TABLE PAINTED TO GIVE A DOUBLE EFFECT OF *FAUX* MARBLE AND *FAUX* WOOD. MAXIME DECORATED THE CHAIRS AND THE ARMOIRES, ONE OF WHICH HOLDS 1930S CROCKERY. THE BUTCHER'S BLOCK WAS FOUND BY MAXIME "IN PIECES" AND REASSEMBLED. DIAMOND INSETS OF GREEN TILE ENLIVEN A FLOOR MADE OF STONE FROM A DISUSED QUARRY IN BARBENTANE.

ABOVE: IN THE "WORKING KITCHEN" EVERY CUPBOARD DOOR HAS RECEIVED MAXIME'S ATTENTION. THE WOODEN CUT OUT ANIMALS ARE CHOPPING BOARDS DESIGNED BY HER SON, ALEXIS DE LA FALAISE.

ABOVE: IN A GUEST BEDROOM A SYLVIA GUIREY WATERCOLOUR IS FRAMED BY A *LIT À LA POLONAISE* (SPOTTED IN A CHRISTIE'S CATALOGUE) WITH ITS ORIGINAL WATERED-VELVET BROCADE INTACT. AN AFRICAN PRINT COVERING THE SOFA CAME FROM A MARKET IN PARIS. THE TWO SMALL ENGLISH PUB TABLES ARE AUTHENTIC.

BELOW: AN ANTIQUE ROLL-TOP BATH TUB SPLENDIDLY RESTORED BY AN ENGLISH COMPANY, WALCOT RECLAMATION OF BATH, IS THE MAIN FEATURE OF A GUEST BATHROOM. THE CHAIR TO THE RIGHT—INEVITABLY—WAS PAINTED BY MAXIME, WHO ALSO DESIGNED THE PATTERN FOR THE FLOOR OF CAROCIM TILES.

RIGHT: IN THE LIVING ROOM BRILLIANT FABRICS BY JOHN STEFANIDIS COVER TWO SOFAS IMPORTED FROM GEORGE SMITH IN LONDON'S KING'S ROAD. ENDLESSLY CREATIVE, MAXIME DESIGNED THE CHRISTOPHER FARR RUG AND MADE THE 'LOVE' LAMPSHADE FROM AN YVES ST LAURENT POSTER, AS WELL AS PAINTING THE COMMODES ON EITHER SIDE OF THE FIREPLACE. THE PAINTED TEA CHESTS BENEATH THE MANTELPIECE ARE CHINESE, FROM THE NINETEENTH CENTURY.

*L*EFT: "CALIFORNIAN LOUIS PHILIPPE" IS MAXIME'S DESCRIPTION OF A CHAIR SHE BOUGHT FOR "PRACTICALLY NOTHING" AND REUPHOLSTERED IN VIBRANT AFRICAN PRINTS, WHICH NOW BEAUTIFULLY COMPLEMENTS THE CHEST OF DRAWERS SHE PAINTED. A MOROCCAN WALLHANGING SERVES AS THE BEDCOVER WHILE THE CURTAINS, MADE OF COTTON VOILE, ARE FROM INDIA. THE BEDSIDE TABLE WAS DESIGNED BY SYRIE MAUGHAM.

RIGHT: IN ANOTHER PRINCIPAL BEDROOM MAXIME COVERED AMERICAN EMPIRE ARMCHAIRS IN "A MIXTURE OF AFRICAN PRINTS AND CRAZY BITS OF FABRIC FROM MY MOTHER'S OLD TRUNKS". THE CHAISE LONGUE WAS A BARGAIN FROM A FLEA MARKET IN NEW YORK CITY, THE NINETEENTH-CENTURY BLUE-GRAY PROVENÇAL CHEST OF DRAWERS WAS FOUND IN L'ISLE-SUR-LA-SORGUE, AND THE CARVED LAUREL-LEAF PILLARS ON EITHER SIDE OF THE FRENCH WINDOWS WERE BOUGHT AT THE OLYMPIA ANTIQUES FAIR IN LONDON. THE FLOOR IS PAVED WITH TERRACOTTA TILES FROM SPAIN.

*A*bove: *Poterie de Cliousclat*
from the Drôme *département* sits on an
Indian metal table, set beside an antique Kashmiri shawl.

Right: Sand taken from a nearby
riverbed to make the render gives the
high walls of the dining room a pinkish tinge. The table was designed by
James Hunter together with a local
ébéniste, who made it from bleached
walnut patinated "to give soul". The
wicker chairs are from Southeast Asia,
the terracotta *jarre* from Greece.
Model sailboats found in Vietnam and
Tripoli, a nineteenth-century oil
seascape and seagrass matting on the
floor suggest a maritime theme.

UNDERSTATED STYLE

On most mornings it is the aroma of baking bread that wakes
Marine Corre. Sometimes too impatient to dress, she will slip on a
coat and follow the mouthwatering smell through the streets of an
unspoiled village to what may well be the best *boulangerie* in the
Lubéron, returning with breakfast to a house that dates back 600
years in parts. Filled with light and imbued with the sense of spaciousness, the house expresses a refreshing modern ethos perfectly.

It was in 1987 that Marine's partner, Jim Hunter, left a busy architectural practice in England to provide designs for and direct
the restoration of Provençal houses, working more on site than on
a drawing board, with a small group of craftsmen who use local
materials and traditional techniques. Like Marine, who with her
sister owns an interior design shop in L'Isle-sur-la-Sorgue, Jim pays
little heed to passing notions of what is "fashionable" in Provence.
His imaginative designs are original, and first and foremost functional—and, as their own home clearly demonstrates, no less beautiful for that.

In the tall square dining room, fashioned from an adjoining ruin, an ancient stone staircase hangs suspended from the ceiling in
mid-air, ingeniously emphasizing the room's remarkable height.
Generous windows provide a view of a flower-filled courtyard,
while the neutral hues of a stone floor and seagrass matting, combined with the subtle pinkish tinge of the walls, add to the feeling
of airy tranquility.

It is a theme repeated throughout the rest of the house: a mix of
predominantly neutral colors, understated furnishings and abundant
natural light. Even the once-gloomy attic, where skeins of silk used
to be hung to dry, is now a sun-filled studio for Marine, with skylights and floor-to-ceiling glass doors leading to a terrace cut into the
roof. The occasional splashes of vibrant color that Marine has introduced—as she does in her shop—come not from Provence but from
gorgeous fabrics that are handpainted especially for her in India, or
handwoven cloth that she finds on annual buying expeditions to far-
flung places in Africa, Central America and the Far East.

Just as Marine and Jim firmly resist the fads of Provence, so the
village in which they live—"Cubist and rather austere"—remains
stubbornly "unfashionable". It suits them perfectly, blessed with the
gift of light—and the most delicious bread in the Lubéron.

LEFT: AN INDIGO-DYED NIGERIAN BATIK MADE AT THE BEGINNING OF THE CENTURY PROVIDES A DRAMATIC BACKDROP FOR MARINE AND JIM'S PREDOMINANTLY WHITE BEDROOM. MARINE FOUND THE ANTIQUE QUILT IN THE NORTH OF ENGLAND, AND MADE THE CURTAINS FROM A PORTUGUESE COTTON PIQUÉ BEDSPREAD. THE CHEST OF DRAWERS IS ENGLISH, AND THE RUG IS PERSIAN.

RIGHT: IN MARINE'S LIGHT-FILLED STUDIO, USED FOR BREAKFASTS AND LUNCHES IN THE WINTER, A WROUGHT-IRON COUNTRY BED FROM HER MOTHER'S ATTIC IS SPREAD WITH AN ANTIQUE INDIAN PATCHWORK, AND BACKED WITH CUSHIONS THAT MARINE COVERED WITH EMBROIDERED FABRIC FROM RAJASTHAN. THE PRINTED BEDSPREAD ENVELOPING THE TABLE UNDER THE SKYLIGHT IS ALSO FROM RAJASTHAN. THE TABLE LAMP IS MADE FROM AN ETHIOPIAN BASKET, LINED WITH OILSKIN THAT WAS USED TO CARRY MILK. ON A "SLIGHTLY SHABBY" TURKISH KILIM A NINETEENTH-CENTURY ENGLISH CANE-BACKED CHAIR CONVERSES ACROSS A *ROTIN* TABLE WITH A CONTEMPORARY CHAIR MADE IN PROVENCE.

Above: The mellow exterior of Nall's and Tuscia's peaceful 350-year-old farmhouse with pink tiled roof. The Greek pithoi date from the eighteenth and nineteenth centuries. Right: Surrounded by the nature that inspires him, Nall creates another fantastic work. He believes in art coexisting with the harmony of nature.

Eclectic Éclat

A dispute with his wealthy father over his wish to be an artist led a young man from Alabama to become known only as Nall, his mother's maiden name. Determined to be self-reliant, he took up his satchel and watercolors and "painted my way around the world". Nall also learnt to be a sculptor, a glassmaker and a silversmith, and for two years he studied under Salvador Dali. Now, some twenty-five years later, the result of a passion driven by necessity is a rich profusion of art that takes your breath away.

Symbolist and baroque, his creations and works in progress cover almost every square inch of his studio, while their style and spirit permeates Nall's small doll-like house, in an extraordinary juxtaposition with the simplicity of its surroundings: twelve acres of grounds stretching over wooded hillsides near the town of Vence.

Elegant furniture, silk-lined walls and Turkish rugs indicate the influence of his Anglo-Italian wife, Tuscia, but it is the eclectic images that Nall creates prolifically and collects that most demand attention: fantastical mosaic landscapes framed in 18 carat gold, and sun-shaped mirrors; antique wax-faced dolls that have sometimes served as his models (for, among others, Christ); the skulls and bones of mammals that for Nall represent "the structure of life"; a richly colored glass pomegranate designed by Nall and handblown in Murano; a bathroom door he encrusted with a pattern of Coca-Cola bottle tops. Most striking of all are Nall's exquisite drawings. Spanning one wall of the dining room, for example, is a "pencil painting" of *The Last Supper* in graphite on Bristol board, with touches of watercolor, pen and ink and human hair, while nearby is a surreal depiction of Tuscia as a Velázquez-style infanta, with Nall's severed head held in her lobster claw.

Nall collects other artists' work as avidly as he paints, and he and Tuscia have established an art association to attract visiting painters, sculptors, novelists, playwrights, and composers from all over the world, who live and work for up to six months in cottages and cabins scattered around the estate. Soon there will be an amphitheatre in which to stage plays and concerts, and a museum-cum-gallery for exhibitions. Looking out over a stunning landscape, Nall reflects with pleasure on what he has created. "I've taken the idea of a small painting and turned it into a way of life."

*A*BOVE: IN NALL'S STUDIO THE PAINTING ON THE WALL IS A WORK IN THE STYLE HE CALLS "NEW ORIENTALISM", WITH A FRAME ENCRUSTED WITH PIECES OF CARPET, WOOD AND COLOURED STONES.

BELOW: A SUMPTUOUS BAROQUE FRAME SURROUNDS A PAINTING OF VENICE. DOLLS HAVE BEEN AN INSPIRATION FOR NALL SINCE THE MID-SEVENTIES, WHEN HE FOUND TWO ANTIQUE DOLLS IN ALABAMA AND STARTED USING THEM AS MODELS.

RIGHT: IN THE DINING ROOM THE TABLE IS SET FOR A LUNCH WITH FRIENDS: THE PORCELAIN DINNER SERVICE, CALLED "METAMORPHOSIS OF A ROSE", WAS DE-SIGNED BY NALL FOR LIMOGES. THE SÈVRES PORCELAIN CHANDELIER CAME FROM TUSCIA'S ITALIAN GRANDMOTHER'S ESTATE IN PARMA.

*A*BOVE LEFT: PORTUGUESE, FRENCH, ITALIAN AND DELFT TILES DECORATE THE INTERIOR STAIRCASE.

BELOW LEFT: AT THE ENTRANCE TO THE HOUSE NALL DESIGNED AND BUILT A MOSAIC USING A MIXTURE OF CARRARA MARBLE, EIGHTEENTH-CENTURY TERRACOTTA AND FRENCH ART DECO TILES.

BELOW: PART OF NALL'S COLLECTION OF ANTIQUE RELIGIOUS FIGURES.

RIGHT: THE WALLS OF THE "RED BEDROOM" WERE SANDED THEN PAINTED CRIMSON WITH SIX COATS OF PAINT, AND HUNG WITH AN ECLECTIC COLLECTION OF FRAMED PRINTS, DRAWINGS AND OIL PAINTINGS.

*A*bove: A stone table and bench have stood in this shady spot for as long as anyone can remember. The two chairs were made of timbers from *HMS Ganges*, the last wooden ship built for the Royal Navy in 1821. In the background is one of several densely planted pergolas.

Right: William with Puck and Pinky, two of his three Jack Russell terriers, in the formal section of the garden at the bottom of Uncle Humphrey's water staircase. He is surrounded by cypresses and kumquat, and (on the left) the long spiky leaves of a strelitzia, or bird of paradise.

BOTANICAL WONDERLAND

Between the Italian border and the villa that was once the beloved home of Katherine Mansfield, the Clos du Peyronnet, with its peeling apricot-colored walls and dark green shutters, stands in an acre of grounds above the town of Menton. In this idyllic spot that enjoys the warmest winters in France, the man they call "the last of his breed"—the last English plantsman on the Riviera—continues a family tradition. It was William Waterfield's grandparents who bought the stately Italianate villa in 1915, and William's Uncle Humphrey who was the principal architect of its extraordinary garden. The property eventually passed to William, and in 1976 he left his job as a lexicographer for the *Oxford English Dictionary* to devote his life to preserving this unique jewel.

But he has achieved far more than that. Whilst it was Uncle Humphrey, with his love of vistas, who devised the stairways and terraces that wind around and up behind the villa, and the artfully placed grotto that suddenly reveals itself, and—his most dramatic fancy—a series of ponds that form a water staircase inspired by the Villa d'Este at Tivoli, it is William's passion for collecting unusual plants that has made the garden truly magical.

Supplied by a far-flung network of contacts that stretches from California to central Chile, he has introduced to this balmy corner of Provence a fabulous array of exotica, so that now, amid the clematis and roses, the acacia and mimosa, there is lotus and papyrus from the Nile region. Magnificent Judas trees from Eurasia and Kashmir cypress keep harmonious company with giant bamboo and eight varieties of avocado. A tamarillo, or tree tomato native to the Peruvian Andes, and a rare strawberry guava complement a fine jacaranda and what William calls "the biggest honeysuckle in the world". There is *Amaryllis belladonna*, and tropical blue waterlilies that float on Uncle Humphrey's ponds, and, in terracotta pots, a "serious collection" of uncommon species including Arabian *Catha edulis* and a splendid example of *Mahonia Siamensis* from Siam.

In this botanical wonderland a "friendly" snake lives in a *jarre* on the topmost terrace, from where you can best appreciate how brilliantly William succeeds in his mission not merely to preserve and enhance but "to *épater*"—to amaze.

ABOVE: ON THE VERANDA FACING WEST, WHERE FLOWERING JASMINE PROVIDES THE CANOPY, SHAFTS OF SUNLIGHT ILLUMINATE THE LEAVES OF AN *AGAVE AMERICANA*, ONE OF WILLIAM'S VAST COLLECTION OF EXOTIC SPECIES.

BELOW: PURPLE *IRIS GERMANICA*.

RIGHT: A MAGNIFICENT WISTERIA THAT IS EIGHTY YEARS OLD FORMS A ROOF FOR THE VERANDA AT THE FRONT OF THE VILLA, ITS GNARLED TRUNK AND BRANCHES CLIMBING THE STONE PILLARS LIKE A VINE. IT FLOWERS EACH APRIL, FORMING A PURPLE CANOPY THAT TONES WITH THE INTENSE BLUE OF THE MEDITERRANEAN SKY. THE "VERY OLD" RIVIERA ROSE IS CALLED "GÉNÉRAL SCHABLIKINE".

ABOVE: TANIA AT WORK IN THE LUSH GARDEN OF HER VILLA.

RIGHT: "A SPOOF OF A TYPICALLY FRENCH EIGHTEENTH-CENTURY ROCOCO CONCEIT," IS HOW TANIA DESCRIBES ONE OF HER EXQUISITELY PAINTED SCREENS IN THE LIVING ROOM. THE MEN'S FACES IN THE LOWER HALF OF THE PANELS WERE INSPIRED BY MEDIEVAL STONE MASONRY. TANIA DESIGNED THE SOFA FABRIC IN A "FADED *TÊTE DE NÈGRE* COLOR" AND PAINTED THE MASONITE TOP OF THE SMALL SIDE TABLE TO MAKE IT LOOK LACQUERED IN WHAT SHE CALLS "A JAPANESERIE STYLE".

Painted dolphins frolic on the lintel of the front door of Tania Vartan's Riviera apartment, as though it were a temple to trompe-l'oeil. In the hallway stenciled carnations in three shades of gold leaf share the walls with giant urns that look as though they were stolen at midnight from a Roman *giardino segreto*. Overhead, glittering stars and a golden sun speckle a deep blue ceiling. Two folding screens with chinoiserie designs appear to be made of blue and white porcelain, while doors are painted a *faux* tortoiseshell. The effect is breathtaking, yet the hallway offers merely a prelude to the house of illusion that Tania has created.

Using scumble glaze and "a hundred different tools"—brushes, of course, but also windscreen wipers, plastic bags, Q-Tips, feathers, crumpled newspapers—Tania has elaborately decorated almost every square inch of her apartment, fabricating an endless variety of "fantasy finishes" including wood, lapis, malachite and marble. Using trompe-l'oeil techniques that twice a year bring students from all over the world to her door for two-week courses she has contrived stunning images in shimmering cool pastels: on her headboard, for example, two swans are joined together in the shape of a lute, made to look as if they are "floating in the heavens". In the living room ethereal clouds appear to hover below the pale blue ceiling and horses gallop over sofa fabric. Landscapes, murals and still lifes, many of them startlingly realistic, grace every wall.

Tania's work also graces many a fashionable apartment in New York, where she was a much sought after artist throughout the 1980s until she tired of city life. A country woman at heart, accustomed to the horses and bluegrass of her native Kentucky, she completed her last American commission—for the White House—in 1989, then looked around for somewhere "more agreeable" to live. It was evocative descriptions of the Côte d'Azur by F. Scott Fitzgerald and Noël Coward that brought her to Provence and, eventually, to the apartment in a gracious villa where she now lives, certain that it is where she truly "belongs".

In that lush setting, influenced by Italian artists of the Renaissance and the French rococo painter Fragonard, and inspired by frequent visits to the great palaces of Europe—"my passion in life"—Tania works ceaselessly, refining her mastery of the art of illusion.

*A*BOVE: ON A GLASS-TOPPED TABLE IN TANIA'S LIVING ROOM ONE OF HER PAINTINGS MIRRORS THE OBJECTS THEM-SELVES: NINETEENTH-CENTURY CHINESE PORCELAIN SHE BOUGHT IN NANKING, AND EMBROIDERED SLIPPERS FOR BOUND FEET. BELOW: TANIA PAINTED AND WAXED THESE TROMPE-L'OEIL ENVELOPES ON THE TERRAZZO ENTRANCE HALL FLOOR OF HER APARTMENT, "SO YOU KNOW WHERE YOU ARE". RIGHT: TWO OF TANIA'S CHINOISERIE-STYLE PAINTED SCREENS SHOW VIGNETTES FROM BOUCHER ENGRAVINGS OF CHINESE PEOPLE. THE BOTTOM HALVES OF THE PANELS ARE "REMINISCENT OF CHIPPENDALE CHINOIS-ERIE". THE PAINTING IS THE FIRST STILL LIFE FROM HER DAYS STUDYING IN FLORENCE, SET ON AN EASEL SHE COVERED WITH MOTIFS INSPIRED BY A BOOK ON *TÔLE* PAINTING TECHNIQUES. SHE DECORATED THE WALLS OF THE ENTRANCE HALL WITH AN OIL GLAZE, THEN STENCILED "SORT OF PERSIAN CARNATIONS" IN GOLD PAINT. HER BEDROOM DOOR HAS THE SAME GLAZE AS THE WALLS, BUT FINISHED WITH A *STRIÉ* PAINT EFFECT.

ABOVE: Around the kitchen fireplace are some of Laurence's collection of *art populaire*—functional objects that are also beautiful—including a fish trap in the shape of a bottle, and green Biot pottery from the 1950s. The objects she collects have no great monetary value: "The value is that I like them".

RIGHT: Much-used hats cluster on a wrought-iron hat-stand that Laurence found in L'Isle-sur-la-Sorgue. On a nineteenth-century Provençal table is what Laurence calls her 'musical piece', a sculpture she made in the U.S.A. in 1979. Bronze, colored black and edged with natural bronze, on a black marble base, it echoes the curves of the hats.

Standing serenely in a *jardin de curé* (a "priest's garden"), the home of Laurence and David Ambrose is a successful marriage between a stone farmhouse, built some 300 years ago, and a *maison de maître* (a "gentleman's house"), added a century or so later. Encircled by rust-red railings, with a handsome gate set in stone pillars, it seems to be waiting for a horse and carriage to sweep up the drive...except that there is no drive leading to the gate, nor even a road—only meadows where once there were vineyards. This is a house that had been sleeping for many years until Laurence brought it wonderfully to life.

An artist and sculptress who insists she is "unknown", Laurence had renovated houses before, though nothing so large and seemingly uninhabitable. But since her chosen architect "wanted everything to be round", she took on the daunting task of designing the renewal herself, and the mixed blessings of daily dealings with Provençal builders.

She succeeded brilliantly, not least because of her unerring sense of scale. In opening up the ground floor with grand gestures she was ever careful to retain its noble symmetry. Under a soaring ceiling in the light-filled living room, where a two-tier stone fireplace is perfectly proportioned, a sweeping staircase leads to a long mezzanine, providing a sense of both spaciousness and intimacy. Her success also lies in her eye for exquisite detail. In designing the staircase, for example, Laurence integrated a tiny circle into each of the balusters of the iron handrail, softening the line and adding grace.

One wing of the house is devoted to the continuing pursuit of creativity. Upstairs Laurence has her studio where she works every day, while downstairs David leads a "monastic life" writing screenplays for Hollywood, scripts for television, plays for the stage and, with increasing frequency, marvelously constructed novels. From the glass-topped desk in his study he has distracting views of the enchanting garden that Laurence planned; next to the study is an exercise room where he fights "writer's sag".

Although the couple spend time in Switzerland, where Laurence was born, or London, where she and David met, Provence is where they most love to be—because of "its excessive weather", the "happiness" of the house, and, above all the endless inspiration their surroundings clearly provide.

𝓛EFT: DISCOVERED IN ST-
RÉMY, THE FIREPLACE WAS ADAPTED BY
LAURENCE TO SUIT THE PROPORTIONS OF
THE ELEGANT LIVING ROOM AND THE CURVE
OF THE STAIRCASE THAT SHE DESIGNED.
RESPLENDENT ABOVE A SOFA COVERED IN
LINEN, THE VENETIAN MIRROR WAS FOUND
IN LONDON. AT THE TOP OF THE STAIRS
HANGS A FLEMISH INTERIOR OF A GOTHIC
CHURCH, PAINTED ON TILES.

RIGHT: A CHESTERFIELD SOFA THAT TRAV-
ELED FIRST FROM FRANCE TO ENGLAND,
THEN BACK TO FRANCE BEFORE LAURENCE
BOUGHT IT IN MONTÉLIMAR, IS NOW THE FA-
VORITE SIESTA SPOT FOR THE AMBROSES'
CAT, LUCIFER (ALSO KNOWN AS LULU).
ABOVE THE SOFA, SET IN A METAL FRAME,
HANG TWO WORKS FROM A SERIES THAT
LAURENCE DID WITH INDIAN INK AND WAX
ON PAPER IN 1994. SHE SAYS SHE WAS IN-
FLUENCED BY BOTH LANDSCAPE AND *NATURE
MORTE*. SHE DOESN'T SET OUT TO BE AB-
STRACT: "YOU START WITH YOUR FEELINGS".

ABOVE: UNDER A LIME TREE IN THE 'PRIEST'S GARDEN' DAISY, THE GUARDIAN OF THE HOUSE, MINDS A CHAISE LONGUE UP-HOLSTERED WITH OLD MATTRESS FABRIC.

BELOW: LAURENCE'S "CONVERSATION PIECE", IN COPPER TREATED TO LOOK LIKE BRONZE, WAS MADE AT A TIME WHEN SHE DID A LOT OF FIGURATIVE WORK OF WOMEN. BEHIND, A POND BUILT WITH OLD STONE IS HOME TO "MILLIONS" OF FROGS.

RIGHT: DELICATE COTTON CURTAINS THAT LAURENCE FOUND IN A FLEA MARKET HANG IN THE GUEST ROOM. A TYPICALLY PROVENÇAL PAINTED TABLE STANDS AGAINST THE BACK WALL, BENEATH A MOROCCAN SCENE FROM THE 1930S. THE BASKETWORK CHAIR IS DATED 1910; THE DECOY BIRD IN THE FOREGROUND IS ENGLISH.

VINTAGE CHARM

The cupboard where spices are kept in Richard Olney's Provençal kitchen is made from old cases that once held bottles of Château Latour, while in his aviary tropical birds make their nests in crates from Château d'Yquem. This is a man with a serious regard for fine French wines—an esteem that is clearly returned by their producers. For in the garden, in an underground *cave* that Richard laboriously created, there is a profound tribute to this expatriate son of Marathon, Iowa: a priceless collection of wines awarded by the Académie du Vin de France in recognition of "*l'ensemble de son œuvre*" ("the body of his work").

Such a prize was richly deserved, for that oeuvre includes his books *Yquem*, *Simple French Food* and *The Good Cook* (*Time-Life's* series on food and wine that, in twenty-seven volumes produced between 1977 and 1982, set out to demystify gastronomy). "Keep it simple, simple, simple" was the underlying philosophy, a tenet that also perfectly describes the chosen manner of his life.

Probably the most knowledgeable gourmet of his era, Richard lives in almost monastic isolation in a small stuccoed, red-roofed house bought more than thirty years ago for $2,000 and restored with what the French describe as "respect for the walls", meaning minimally. Set in a former quarry, it overlooks an unspoiled village where the streets are "regularly blocked by the insouciant passage of the shepherd and his troop". He has no television or car and depends on a part-time gardener to drive him once a week to the markets of Toulon. Otherwise he glories in the self-sufficiency of his garden, where he grows tomatoes, onions and shallots, tiny tender lettuces, tarragon and hyssop for salads that might be flavored with wine vinegar that he makes himself in a *vinaigrier*. In the spring the nearby hillsides provide wild asparagus that he picks and parboils "for just two seconds" to provide the filling for omelets made with eggs laid by his own chickens. Then there are the *daubes* he makes in an old black earthenware pot imbued with the delicious aromas of olive oil and garlic that "give of themselves time and again".

For several hours each day, steadily but slowly on an old manual typewriter that "goes at the same rate I do", he writes lovingly of food "that does not argue with the wine". His next book has no deadline, for now he must make time for the simple pleasures of his tranquil life.

ABOVE: RICHARD'S WINE CELLAR IN HIS GARDEN TOOK TWO YEARS OF DIGGING AND BUILDING TO MAKE. IT CONTAINS VINTAGES THAT INCLUDES YQUEM AND TEMPIER, AND TAYLOR'S PORT FROM 1927, ALL LAID ON STONE SHELVES.

RIGHT: IN THE KITCHEN OF THE HOUSE RICHARD BOUGHT FOR $2,000 MORE THAN THIRTY YEARS AGO, THE FIREPLACE IS THE DOMINANT FEATURE. ON AND AROUND IT HE KEEPS HIS MORTARS AND PESTLES, AND COPPER AND CAST-IRON PANS. IN PLANNING THE KITCHEN, HE SAYS, "I JUST DID WHAT SEEMED INEVITABLE."

*A*BOVE: RATATOUILLE MADE TWO YEARS EARLIER AND STORED IN A STERILIZED JAR, GLOWING WITH THE COLORS OF PROVENCE AND DECORATED WITH FRESH BASIL LEAVES. RICHARD GROWS HIS OWN HERBS, AND PLANTS A DIFFERENT VARIETY OF TOMATO EVERY YEAR BECAUSE HE'S NEVER SATISFIED WITH THE FLAVOR.

BELOW: SARDINES THAT RICHARD FILLETS THEN DIPS IN LEMON JUICE WITH GROUND COARSE SEA SALT AND PEPPER, AND PARSLEY AS A GARNISH AND A GENEROUS AMOUNT OF FRUITY LOCAL OLIVE OIL POURED OVER. THEY ARE EATEN RAW—"MORE DIGESTIBLE", ACCORDING TO RICHARD.

RIGHT: RICHARD FINDS WONDERFUL FRESH FISH AT THE MARKET IN TOULON; HERE, A *DAURADE ROSE*, A SORT OF BREAM, CLEANED BUT WITH ITS HEAD AND TAIL INTACT. IT IS PREPARED WITH FINELY SLICED ONIONS AND GARLIC, OLIVE OIL AND WHITE WINE, WITH FRESH WILD FENNEL TUCKED UNDERNEATH, AND BAKED IN THE OVEN.

PROVENCE RESTORED

Uninhabited for thirty years, the forester's cottage stood neglected amid an overgrown walled garden in an otherwise immaculate hamlet, looking "unbearably sad"—the more so after one of the walls was partially demolished by a runaway truck and not repaired. Yet as Michael van Gessel, Arjan Schipper and Cees Pronk learned when, imagining how the ruin might be given new life, they sought to buy it, the bond between some Provençaux and their land is so strong that they refuse to sell even what they have abandoned. Only after three years of persuasion did the owner agree to part with the cottage, and then not for cash but *en viager* (in return for a life annuity). "Sold" said the trio, despite the complications of the arrangement, and at last the rebirth could begin.

They set about the renovation with painstaking care, resolved to "respect the integrity of its spaces" and determined that most of the materials used, and all of the furnishings, should come from Provence. Thus, while local craftsmen made the kitchen cabinets by hand, and skilfully restored the French oak floor in the summer kitchen and dining room, Michael, Arjan and Cees never missed an opportunity—on flying visits from their homes in Amsterdam—to scour the area's antiques markets and *brocantes*. Now, they say with pride, almost every single object in the house is French-made, down to the very last wine glass.

The once-unkempt garden is now lovingly tended, a palette of ever-changing colors. At Christmas the first flowers appear, roses with wide greenish-white petals. By March the garden is carpeted with yellow daffodils, followed by scented *Narcissus poeticus*. Next come blue aquilegia, then bright blue iris, then white lilies, then lavender. The purple theme is repeated in August with verbena, which gives way in its turn to white Japanese anemones. An expanse of *Aster* "Monte Casino", with tiny white flowers, provides the year's shimmering finale.

The house has been redesigned as a sanctuary for three men with busy lives, but also for communal living, for it is often visited by legions of friends and family who gather in one of the two large kitchens—one for summer, the other for winter—for endless meals and conversation. With its shutters painted in *gris flamand* that turns a subtle blue in the Provençal light, the once-sad house now stands joyously in its delightful garden, awaiting arrivals for the next celebration.

*L*EFT: MICHAEL VAN GESSEL, THE GARDEN'S DESIGNER, PROMISED "IT WILL BE BEAUTIFUL"—AND HE WAS RIGHT. IT IS PLANTED IN A PALETTE OF COLORS, WITH BLUE, YELLOW AND WHITE FLOWERS THAT ALSO GROW WILD IN THE AREA.
ABOVE: THE OLD VINES PRODUCE GRAPES FROM WHICH THE FRIENDS MAKE *SAUTEL*, A LOCAL DRINK. SUGAR AND HERBS ARE ADDED TO THE GRAPE JUICE, THEN LEFT TO FERMENT UNTIL A "WONDERFUL APÉRITIF FOR THE REST OF THE YEAR" IS READY AROUND CHRISTMAS. THE GARDEN FURNITURE WAS FOUND IN *BROCANTES* AND PAINTED IN A MEDLEY OF GREENS.

*L*EFT: THE WRITING DESK IN A CORNER OF ONE OF THE TWO KITCHENS CAME FROM A *BROCANTE* IN THE AREA. THE FIREPLACE IS USED EVERY DAY IN THE SPRING, AUTUMN AND WINTER. THE FLOORS ARE MADE OF OLD FRENCH OAK, REPAIRED AND RESTORED.

RIGHT: THE KITCHEN WAS ORIGINALLY A STORAGE SPACE FOR HAY, IN THE DAYS WHEN THIS PART OF THE HOUSE WAS USED FOR STABLING HORSES. IT WAS CONVERTED AND FURNISHED WITH ENORMOUS CARE, HARNESSING THE SKILLS OF A LOCAL CRAFTSMAN WHO DOES NOTHING BUT RESTORE HOUSES FOR A LIVING. CARE WAS TAKEN, TOO, WITH THE GOLDEN-OCHRE COLOR SCHEME—INSPIRED BY VISITS TO MONT VENTOUX—AND THE PAINTWORK OF THE HANDMADE CABINETS. IT IS A ROOM FOR BEING SOCIABLE AND MAKING LOCAL DISHES IN: "BIG PIECES OF MEAT, FRENCH SOUPS, FANTASTIC SALADS".

*A*BOVE: A SEVENTEENTH-CEN-
TURY BENCH IN THE GARDEN SUPPORTS AN
EIGHTEENTH-CENTURY MARBLE BUST DEPICT-
ING MARIE ANTOÏNETTE.
RIGHT: TWO CAVALIER KING CHARLES
SPANIELS, THE HOUSE DOGS PANTOUFLÉ AND
BABY MANON, POSE ON A LOUIS XVI *LIT À
LA POLONAISE.* THE FABRIC DATES FROM
AROUND 1850. THE PAINTING—ONE OF
LILLIAN'S "WITNESSES OF TIME"—IS OF AN
EIGHTEENTH-CENTURY PROVENÇAL WOMAN
HOLDING ROSES IN HER HANDS—A SIGN
THAT SHE IS READY FOR MARRIAGE.

Ever since she played Mozart on the piano—"badly"—as a child, and was sent home from school for wearing unfashionably long dresses, and chose the memoirs of the Comte de Tilly as her bedtime reading, Lillian Williams has lived in a different time. She should have been born some 250 years ago—and not in Klemath Falls, Oregon, but in France. The Pavillon de Bidaine, set deep in the Provençal countryside, is her breathtaking recreation of the eighteenth century she not only prefers but adores. Approached through colossal gates, adorned by majestic gardens, grottoes and a succession of fountains and ornamental pools, this former hunting lodge provides abundant evidence of her chosen mission in life: her magnificent obsession "to save the past".

A classic seventeenth-century pavilion, the house was lavish in the style of the 1950s when Lillian and her husband, Ted, discovered it. Brocade covered the walls, and layers of heavy curtains were draped at the windows—all far too oppressive for their taste. With flair and boundless energy they set out to transform it into a glorious *folie* of brilliant fabrics and pigments—of cascading curtains and tented ceilings and sumptuous silk canopies, of walls and furniture beautifully painted—filled with the rich echoes of an epoch that ended with the Revolution. It is not so much the grand and gilded furniture of that era that intrigues Lillian, though she owns a number of exquisite *lits à la polonaise* including one that belonged to Marie Antoinette, but the statues, portraits ("the witnesses of time"), and other ephemera of eighteenth-century life, such as a servant's cap or a pair of silk stockings.

Above all, antique clothes and fabrics, the whites laid out to bleach in the Provençal sun, are an abiding passion. Lillian's collection of fabrics is vast, and her period costumes have been frequently exhibited at the New York Metropolitan Museum of Art. Yet, in decorating the house, she successfully mixed old with new, using the vivid prints of her friend the late Laura Ashley, and her own designs, copied from her fabric collection, to achieve some of her most stunning settings.

Surrounded by more than thirty King Charles spaniels, Lillian and Ted live a life as far removed as possible from the twentieth century, in the place where they were surely meant to be. As Lillian says, "Houses, like marriages, have their destiny."

*A*BOVE: IN THE *FEMME DE CHAMBRE*'S ROOM AN ALCOVE BED IS COVERED WITH ORIGINAL EIGHTEENTH-CENTURY *TOILE DE NANTES* PRINTED COTTON, FOUND IN THE HOUSE. THE *FAUTEUIL* IN THE FOREGROUND, COVERED WITH EIGHTEENTH-CENTURY *TOILE DE ROUEN*, FACES A PROVENÇAL CHAIR FROM THE SAME EPOCH.

BELOW: IN THE CHINESE SALON A PIEDMONTESE PAINTED TABLE FLANKS A LOUIS XV *LIT DE REPOS* COVERED IN COTTON *BROCATELLE*. THE EIGHTEENTH-CENTURY CLOCK (ON THE RIGHT) IS A FAKE MADE FOR THE THEATRE AND HAS ALWAYS TOLD THE SAME TIME, JUST AS FOR LILLIAN AND TED "TIME STOPS IN THE EIGHTEENTH CENTURY".

RIGHT: THE *BLANCHISSERIE* IS THE ORIGINAL LAUNDRY ROOM OF THE HOUSE, WHERE LILLIAN KEEPS PART OF HER VAST FABRIC COLLECTION ON AN IRONING TABLE COVERED IN STRIPED TOILE. LILLIAN HAND-PAINTED THE WALLS, A STRATEGY WIDELY ADOPTED IN THE EIGHTEENTH CENTURY, WHEN WALLPAPER WAS EXTREMELY COSTLY.

LEFT: THE WALLS, CEILING AND FURNITURE OF A TENTED BEDROOM ARE ALL COVERED IN THE SAME FABRIC, BY LAURA ASHLEY. A *BALDAQUIN*, OR CANOPY, IS SUSPENDED OVER A LOUIS XVI BED. ALSO LOUIS XVI, THE LACQUERED *BERGÈRE* WINGED CHAIR IS ONE OF A PAIR. ON THE WALLS HANG WATERCOLORS OF EIGHTEENTH-CENTURY MEN'S FASHIONS AND, IN AN OVAL FRAME, A PASTEL OF THE FRENCH DAUPHIN.

RIGHT: THE CEILING DECORATION IN THE LIBRARY WAS COPIED FROM CARDINAL RICHELIEU'S SEVENTEENTH-CENTURY HOUSE IN PARIS. THE MANNEQUIN OF A WOMAN DATES FROM THE ITALIAN RENAISSANCE, WHILE THE *SANTONI* (PLASTER STATUES OF SAINTS) IN THE CABINETS ARE NEAPOLITAN, FROM THE 1700S. ON THE TABLE TO THE LEFT IS A COLLECTION OF *MERCURE DE FRANCE*—FRENCH NEWSPAPERS FROM THE PERIOD 1784-93—PART OF THE EPHEMERA OF EIGHTEENTH-CENTURY LIFE THAT SO CAPTIVATES LILLIAN AND TED.

*A*BOVE: THE MAROON AND GOLD WALLPAPER BY THE STAIRCASE IS A LAURA ASHLEY COPY OF A SEVENTEENTH-CENTURY WOODBLOCK; LAURA ASHLEY HERSELF FOUND THE ORIGINAL PATTERN IN A TRUNK IN A CASTLE. FASHION PLATES ON THE WALLS ARE HANDCOLORED LATE-SEVENTEENTH-CENTURY FRENCH ENGRAVINGS SHOWING THE DRESS STYLES OF THE TIME.

BELOW: LILLIAN HAS COLLECTED MORE THAN 200 CHAIRS, SOME GRAND, MOST MORE HUMBLE. WHATEVER THEIR PEDIGREE, SHE SAYS, "CHAIRS SPEAK VOLUMES".

RIGHT: THE LARGE STATUE OF AN ANGEL AT THE BOTTOM OF THE STAIRCASE IS SEVENTEENTH-CENTURY PROVENÇAL, MADE OF GESSOED WOOD. IT STANDS NEXT TO AN ITALIAN PAINTED SPINET FROM THE SAME CENTURY, PART OF TED'S LARGE COLLECTION OF EARLY MUSICAL INSTRUMENTS. A LOUIS XV LANTERN HANGS NEAR A LARGE PORTRAIT OF LOUIS XIV'S CHILDREN, BY SANTERRE, ENTITLED *THE MUSIC LESSON*.

CONRAN'S KINGDOM

It was marvelous serendipity that led Sir Terence Conran to his idea of the perfect home in Provence: the Mas de Brunélys was "modest, not grand", set amid lush fields, cypresses and pines, and—best of all—derelict behind its patchy pink façade, and therefore open to whatever his unique sense of style and design might propose. On the ground floor of the two-story farmhouse he imagined a comfortable living space for winter. In one of the two barns, adjoined at either end, he saw a spacious white and cream kitchen where he would indulge his passion for cooking; in the other, an airy summer living room with polished stone floors and a gray-green beamed ceiling. Above would be the master bedroom with a fireplace and oak floors for warmth in the winter; and running the length of the house, past the guest bedrooms, a corridor through which soft breezes would drift in the summer.

Against all local wisdom born of the *mistral*, he would open up the northern face of the house with doors and windows to fill the house with light. His brilliant impertinence was to imagine an alternative defence against the wind: a steep slope behind the house, landscaped with a terraced garden. It would be graced by a broad flight of weathered gray stone steps, with water staircases falling on either side, leading up to the summit where a swimming pool would be concealed, sheltered by tall cypresses and shaded by plane trees. A hammock would hang there, beneath a bower of vines: a perfect place to think, and draw, and write, and "while away the days".

All that stood between this inspired vision and its realization was a vast amount of work—and the state agency, charged with the preservation of viable estates, which owned the Mas de Brunélys and would choose the most suitable buyer. With only a faint hope, Sir Terence added his name to the list of thirty people who had already applied to buy it, and thought no more about the house until, six months later, he learnt that it was his.

Perhaps he was chosen because he pledged to create his idyll with the utmost sensitivity. When, two years later, a delegation of his neighbors walked up the avenue of horse chestnuts leading to the Mas de Brunélys, to see for themselves what *l'Anglais* had achieved, he was immensely pleased with their reaction: "amazement, tempered with pleasure" that after all the effort and care invested, to their eyes "nothing had changed".

*L*EFT: CLASSIC CONRAN: IN ONE CORNER OF SIR TERENCE'S BEDROOM AN APPLEWOOD TABLE FROM THE CONRAN SHOP IN LONDON PERFECTLY ENCAPSULATES THE TIMELESS QUALITY AND BEAUTIFUL SIMPLICITY OF HIS DESIGN ETHOS.

ABOVE: AN AVENUE OF MAJESTIC HORSE CHESTNUT TREES DRAWS YOU TO THE MAS DE BRUNÉLYS, ITS REDDISH-PINK FAÇADE AND PALE SHUTTERS JUST VISIBLE THROUGH THE FOLIAGE.

*L*EFT: THE SUMMER LIVING ROOM, THAT LOOKS OUT ON TO THE ASTONISHING GARDEN SIR TERENCE HAS CREATED, IS SIMPLY FURNISHED WITH COMFORTABLE SOFAS AND AMPLE ARMCHAIRS. THE TABLE, BEARING A BOWL OF BOULES FOR IMPROMPTU GAMES OF *PÉTANQUE* (BELOW), WAS FORMERLY A DOOR.

RIGHT: IN THE CONVIVIAL KITCHEN, WHERE "A HUGE AMOUNT OF COOKING GOES ON", FAMILY AND FRIENDS CAN GATHER AROUND AN IMMENSE OAK TABLE MADE BY BENCHMARK. THE WORKTABLE, ALSO OAK, AND THE OPEN SHELVING INSPIRED BY ENGLISH DRESSERS, WERE DESIGNED BY SIR TERENCE. THE CHAIRS WERE FOUND LOCALLY. STONE FLOOR TILES FROM CHASSAGNE ARE COOL ON SUMMER DAYS.

*L*EFT: "RIDICULOUSLY GRAND" IS SIR TERENCE'S DESCRIPTION OF THE MAGNIFICENT STONE STAIRCASE HE CREATED IN THE GARDEN, LEADING UP FROM A LILY POND TO THE TOPMOST TERRACE WHERE THE SWIMMING POOL IS HIDDEN. ONE OF HIS GUESTS, THE ARTIST DAVID HOCKNEY, SAID THAT WALKING DOWN THE STAIRCASE, BORDERED BY A CANAL OF RUNNING WATER, MADE HIM FEEL "LIKE NERO".

BELOW: A SHADY PLACE FOR AL FRESCO SUMMER DINING.

RIGHT: GERANIUMS PROSPER IN A TERRACOTTA *JARRE* ON A SUN-DAPPLED PATIO WHERE SIR TERENCE LIKES TO THINK, DRAW AND WRITE. "AROUND ELEVEN O'CLOCK I GET A BOTTLE OF WINE, SIT AT THE TABLE AND WHILE AWAY MY DAY."

The house needed to be large enough to provide 'private spaces' for both the children, and for grandchildren not yet conceived, and for all the friends who would constantly fill it. There needed to be room in the garden for a swimming pool, and for a generous terrace where family and friends could spend long summer days. It had to be set in one of those glorious but unpretentious villages in the lush Comtat-Venaissin where there are but a handful of outsiders, and where once a week the locals fill the square with tables for a communal supper. And, with luck, the woman who ran the tiny *tabac* from the front room of her house might appoint herself the unofficial but ever-vigilant *gardienne*. It took Marie Jourdan, known universally as Mady, four years to find such a house—and "ten minutes" to agree to buy it.

Standing in the heart of a village shaped like a snail's shell, the nineteenth-century farmhouse and outbuildings required considerable restoration, all of it carried out to Mady's plans by local artisans. They included a banker-turned-housepainter who ragged the interior walls with a mixture of linseed oil and pigments from Roussillon, and who endowed the façade with a patina of overlaid hues of ocher, yellow, olive green and straw.

Mady is an antiques dealer with a shop in New York that specializes in nineteenth-century French furniture, and, for the fun of it, "crazy" chandeliers, furniture and decorative objects from the Thirties and Forties. The furniture in her house reflects her exquisite and eclectic taste, but this is no showroom or a place for meeting clients. Rather it is a refuge where Mady catches her breath, and where, above all, she can enjoy the company of her adult children, Antoine and Marie.

Part of the house is set aside for the friends they bring, and part of it for Antoine, who, as Mady admits, is far too tall for a bathroom squeezed under the eaves. In compensation, perhaps, his bedroom has a lofty cathedral ceiling. Marie's private space includes a bedroom that looks on to a garden overflowing with jasmine. One wall is lined with cupboards whose doors came from a convent, one of which opens to reveal a hidden passageway leading to Marie's spacious bathroom and to another room that is beautifully furnished but not yet occupied. This is what will one day complete Mady's "house of joy": what she describes with certainty as "the baby's room-to-be".

ABOVE: IN MADY'S KITCHEN HANDMADE CUPBOARDS, PAINTED A COLOR "BETWEEN OCHER AND MUSTARD", ARE DECORATED WITH WROUGHT-IRON *MOUSTACHES*. THE POTS WITH GLAZED OCHRE LIPS ARE FROM THE SOUTHWEST OF FRANCE, WHILE THE NINETEENTH-CENTURY MILK CHURNS— *POTS À LAIT*—ON THE SECOND SHELF CAME FROM EASTERN FRANCE.

RIGHT: BLUE GINGHAM SEAT PADS ON THE NINETEENTH-CENTURY KITCHEN CHAIRS ECHO THE BLUE OF THE FLOOR TILES. THE EIGHTEENTH-CENTURY CHERRYWOOD DRESSER HOLDS 1950S DIOR PLATES.

*L*EFT: UNDER A WEATHERED ROOF THE OPEN EATING AREA, WITH A NINE- TEENTH-CENTURY FARMHOUSE TABLE AND A CONVENT BENCH, IS "WHERE WE PRACTICAL- LY LIVE IN THE SUMMER". ABOVE THE TABLE MADY HAS SUSPENDED TWO NINETEENTH- CENTURY BIRDCAGES, IN WHICH SHE PLACES SMALL CANDLES THAT PROVIDE ROMANTIC ILLUMINATION ON SUMMER EVENINGS.

RIGHT: THE BACK OF THE HOUSE HAS BEEN PAINTED A PINKY-RED OCHRE, USING ROUSSILLON PIGMENTS, WHILE THE SHUT- TERS ARE A *BLEU CHARRETTE*. THE GARDEN IS ENCHANTING: A SMALL LAWN WITH A SOLITARY OLIVE TREE LEADS UP TO TER- RACES PLANTED WITH A MASS OF ARTI- CHOKES, ROSES, LAUREL AND THYME. A TRELLIS OVERFLOWING WITH JASMINE RUNS THE LENGTH OF THE SWIMMING POOL.

*L*EFT: A TESTER CROWNS THE PAINTED PROVENÇAL BED IN DAUGHTER MARIE'S BEDROOM. THE FRENCH QUILT, BEDSIDE TABLE, LEATHER ARMCHAIR DRAPED WITH AN AMERICAN PATCHWORK, AND CAMPHOR WOOD CHEST ARE ALL NINETEENTH-CENTURY TREASURES.

BELOW: A PEEK INTO "THE BABY'S-ROOM-TO-BE", WITH ITS NINETEENTH-CENTURY SPANISH BED.

RIGHT: IN THE COMBINED DINING AND LIVING ROOM A SEVENTEENTH-CENTURY WOODEN STATUE GRACES AN ITALIAN CHEST FROM THE SAME ERA. A LOUIS XV TABLE IS SET BETWEEN TWO NAPOLEON III ARMCHAIRS.

*A*BOVE: IN ANTOINE'S BATH-ROOM A WOODEN BENCH FROM CONNECTICUT, AN OLIVE JAR, AND AN AMERICAN ADIRONDACK CHAIR—WITH A *COUVERTURE* FROM ARLES OVER ONE ARM—ARE ALL SURVIVORS FROM THE NINETEENTH CENTURY. THE PHOTOGRAPH ON THE BENCH IS A FAMILY PORTRAIT OF MADY'S GREAT-GRANDPARENTS (ANTOINE IS NAMED AFTER HIS GREAT-GRANDFATHER).

BELOW: IN THE MASTER BATHROOM AN EIGHTEENTH-CENTURY *DIRECTOIRE BIDET* CAMOUFLAGED AS A CHAIR CONCEALS A BASIN MADE FROM *PORCELAINE DE ROUEN*.

RIGHT: A 1930S BATHTUB WITH ORNATE LEGS HAS BEEN REPAINTED IN "BORDEAUX".

A SENSE OF SCALE

Though she had every intention of living in Italy, Catharine Warren, an American painter, came to Provence on a whim for the Christmas of 1988, and fell in love with its winter beauty. She came back the following year "just to look", and the first house she saw was the Mas de Mérimbeau, an apricot-colored farmhouse with cream shutters. She knew instantly that it was where she must paint—and not only her exquisite canvases.

Warm, amusing and prodigiously creative, Catharine has fashioned a home that is a kaleidoscope of colors. The walls are painted an intense saffron yellow, or pale pink, or pistachio green. Almost every piece of furniture, discovered in local antique markets, is now painted in one or more of her favorite hues: yellows, olive, "funny grays and greens", and occasional splashes of crimson red—"colours you would never use anywhere else". In the dining room even the canvas curtains framing the windows bear abstract splashes of green and black from her paintbrush.

If her use of color is imaginative and bold, so too is Catharine's choice of furniture and objects—mainly large pieces, for she likes "things that have volume and command space". She happily mixes pieces from the eras of Louis XV, Louis XVI and Napoleon III with "funny little things" from the Thirties and Forties, immense gilded mirrors, and dramatic arrangements of greenery. Because Catharine's sense of scale is unerring, what could look chaotic is instead breathtaking.

No less beautiful, but dreamy rather than dramatic, her garden looks as though it has existed for centuries. Cypress trees surround a series of intimate spaces, separated by evergreen walls of yew and oleander. There is a rose garden framed by gray santolina, with a pergola where Catharine is training more roses to climb. An English-style garden has a bower covered in honeysuckle, bottle-brush trees growing in painted green pots and a small round table and chairs "for afternoon tea".

How Catharine finds time for tea is a mystery, for she paints in her studio every day, tends her garden, entertains large numbers of friends for dinner, and still never ceases to create wonderful new surprises. In her orchard, heady with the scents of almond and apricot, Catharine has conjured up a vast but almost invisible swimming pool that, coloured dark gray and edged with old stone, simply melts into the magical landscape.

*L*EFT: UNDER AN ABUNDANT CHERRY TREE IN HER GARDEN CATHARINE HAS CREATED A SHADED REFUGE FOR COOL DRINKS ON LONG HOT AFTERNOONS. SHE INTENDED TO COVER THE SEAT CUSHIONS OF THE IRON FURNITURE, CIRCA 1940s, WITH WHITE FABRIC, UNTIL SHE ANTICIPATED THE HAVOC OF STAINS THAT FALLING CHERRIES MIGHT MAKE.

TOP AND ABOVE: SCENES FROM AN "ENGLISH GARDEN" IN PROVENCE.

*A*BOVE LEFT: IN THE KITCHEN, BESIDE A GODIN STOVE, CATHARINE "PLANTED" A WOODEN TREE TRELLIS MEANT FOR TRAINING DECORATIVE VINES.

BELOW LEFT: THE STAND HOLDING PLATES AND BOTTLES IS A REPRODUCTION FROM HERVÉ BAUME IN AVIGNON. THE OCHER TOBY JUG AND BOWL ARE CONTEMPORARY.

BELOW: CHERRIES IN A CLASSIC GLAZED OCHRE DISH MADE IN APT, BY AN ANTIQUE *BARBOTINE* JUG.

RIGHT: A NINETEENTH-CENTURY IRON CHAISE LONGUE, WHICH CATHARINE PAINTED GOLD AND COVERED IN FABRIC BY RUBELLI, GRACES THE SALON. THE EIGHTEENTH-CENTURY *PANTALONNIÉRE* HAS DRAWERS SUFFICIENTLY SPACIOUS TO ALLOW GENTLEMEN'S TROUSERS TO BE STORED WITHOUT FOLDING.

*A*BOVE: A WELCOMING BIRD MADE OF PAINTED WOOD AND *TÔLE*, WHICH ONCE SERVED AS A SHOP SIGN, NOW HOVERS NEAR ONE ENTRANCE TO CATHARINE'S KITCHEN; SHE FOUND IT ON ONE OF HER FREQUENT EXPEDITIONS TO THE ANTIQUES MARKETS OF L'ISLE-SUR-LA-SORGUE. THE IRON CHAIR, DISCOVERED IN A SHOP IN NEARBY ST-RÉMY, WAS MADE IN INDIA SOME FIFTY YEARS AGO.

BELOW: CATHARINE'S PAINTBRUSH GAVE NEW LIFE TO AN OLD SCREEN, AND A FRESH YELLOW BACKGROUND TO THE PAINTING OF A BIRD ON GLASS.

RIGHT: EVER INVENTIVE, CATHARINE USED FABRIC BOUGHT IN L'ISLE-SUR-LA-SORGUE TO LINE THE WALLS OF A GUEST BEDROOM, AND TO FASHION THE MATCHING SCREEN. THE RATTAN TABLE AND CHAIRS, AND THE OIL-ON-BOARD STUDY OF A YOUNG GIRL, ARE NINETEENTH CENTURY. THE CONTEMPORARY TERRACOTTA FLOOR TILES ARE HANDMADE.

LEFT: COUNTLESS FORAYS IN THE ANTIQUE SHOPS OF L'ISLE-SUR-LA-SORGUE PRODUCED THE ARRAY OF FURNITURE AND OBJECTS OF DIFFERENT ERAS AND STYLES IN THE SALON, WHERE TERRACOTTA FLOOR TILES HARMONIZE BEAUTIFULLY WITH SAFFRON WALLS. A *FAUX-MARBRE*-TOPPED TABLE DATES FROM THE NINETEENTH CENTURY, WHILE THE CHANDELIER, ADORNED WITH FABRIC POM-POMS, IS LOUIS PHILIPPE. THE ARMCHAIR UPHOLSTERED IN CHINTZ, LIKE THE TWO SOFAS, IS LOUIS XV. CRYSTAL VASES FILLED WITH GREENERY FROM THE GARDEN STAND ATOP NAPOLEON III WOOD *GUÉRIDONS*. ITALIAN CANDELABRA, AND THE TOWERING FRENCH MIRROR THEY FLANK, ARE EIGHTEENTH CENTURY.

RIGHT: BLUE COTTON FABRIC FROM BLANCHET OF CAVAILLON, CATHARINE'S FAVORITE DRAPERY SHOP IN PROVENCE, LINES THE WALLS OF HER DRESSING ROOM. MATTRESS TICKING ON A WROUGHT-IRON CHAIR AND FOOTSTOOL, AND A NINETEENTH-CENTURY IRON BED THAT CATHARINE PAINTED, MATCH IT PERFECTLY. AN EARLY-EIGHTEENTH-CENTURY FRENCH SCREEN WITH CHINESE MOTIFS CROWNS THE EFFECT.

A three-colored dog trained to hunt for boar led the way through a hilltop village, to where a farmer sat beside a shoebox on which he had scribbled in chalk his irresistible proposal: "Ruin for Sale". Actually it was ruins, of four modest seventeenth-century cottages (though one had irretrievably collapsed) and two grottoes cut into the rock, which had provided shelter in much earlier times—all secured on the spot with a down payment of 5,000 francs. And so began, in 1965, through serendipity rather than design, a twenty-five-year labor of love that would employ—off and on, when funds allowed—two generations of *maçons*, and fashion, from what was there rather than what might be imposed, an interlocking labyrinth of vaulted rooms and sheltered courtyards, of steep stone stairs and cool passageways and, on three levels, secret wild gardens with cistus and asphodel—perhaps the only gardens in the entire Lubéron where asphodel grows. Like the landscapes they survey, the interwoven homes of Joe Downing and his companion are a joy to all the senses: an Elysium of Roman tiles, sunshine and the aroma of thyme.

Raised on a tobacco farm in Horse Cave, Kentucky, Joe originally studied optometry—until the love of painting "devoured" him. When he came to France in 1950 it was to have been for only the briefest of visits...but the visit never ended. Encouraged early on in his career by Pablo Picasso, he is, as one critic described him, a "candid visionary" who invariably rises with the dawn and paints for hours on end each day, using a child's high chair as his palette, and surrounded by the legion of stray cats which find refuge in his secret gardens, plus Julie and Jessica, the two dogs he rescued from the local pound.

In what was once a hayloft, perched at the top of a death-defying spiral staircase, where the original residents kept garlic and onions and (because of the warmth rising from the pens of the livestock below) their children, Joe creates kaleidoscopic abstract images on canvas, leather, concrete, antique linens, ancient wooden doors, porcelain, three-dimensional columns, metal and roof tiles, their concavities washed with color. He works with extraordinary patience and intuition, depending on the natural eloquence of oils, allowing one dab of color to call forth the next, until—with his paintings as with his house—he achieves the perfect balance.

*A*BOVE: THREE OF JOE'S COLLECTION OF TRADITIONAL PROVENÇAL POTS STAND IN HIS "YELLOW AND BLUE ROOM DESIGNED FOR EATING WATER MELON", WHICH IS ENTIRELY COVERED WITH MOROCCAN TILES.

RIGHT: IN A STUDIO BUILT INTO THE ROCK AT THE TOP OF HIS HOUSE, JOE DOWNING SETS OUT TO EXPRESS "LIGHT AND HAPPINESS", CREATING FANTASIES OF COLOR THAT MEAN "WHATEVER YOU WANT THEM TO MEAN". IN THE FOREGROUND LIES WHAT WILL BE THE MAIN ELEMENT FOR ONE OF HIS CELEBRATED RAWHIDE SCULPTURES. ONE OF THE COLUMNS HE STANDS BETWEEN IS ALSO MADE OF LEATHER, THE OTHER OF ANTIQUE HEAVY LINEN BEDSHEETS THAT HE FOUND IN THE VILLAGE.

*L*EFT: THE ITALIAN MARBLE
TABLE IN THE DINING ROOM WAS DESIGNED
BY EMMANUEL WARDI. ON THE MANTEL-
PIECE A NINETEENTH-CENTURY CHERRY-
WOOD HORSE, CARVED FOR A FARMER'S
CHILD, STANDS IN FRONT OF A NAIVE TAPES-
TRY BY ROSE DECANE.

ABOVE: A COLLECTION OF EIGHTEENTH-
CENTURY *TOUPEN* USED TO BREW CONCOC-
TIONS OF SAGE, FOR SETTLING STOMACHS.

RIGHT: IN THE ENTRANCE HALL A PLASTER
RELIEF INSPIRED BY DELLA ROBBIA HANGS
ABOVE A NINETEENTH-CENTURY ENGLISH
TABLE. THE CREIL MARBLED BOWL IS NINE-
TEENTH CENTURY.

ABOVE: A CHILD'S HIGH CHAIR, FOUND ABANDONED IN THE VILLAGE, SERVES AS JOE'S PALETTE, ENABLING HIM TO MIX HIS OILS WITHOUT STOOPING.

BELOW: A COMPLETED RAWHIDE SCULPTURE IS BLESSED BY BISHOP PETRONIUS, PATRON SAINT OF BOLOGNA. THE NINETEENTH-CENTURY STATUE, MADE OF POLYCHROME WOOD, WAS COATED WITH GESSO, PAINTED WITH OILS, AND GILDED.

RIGHT: ON PALE TERRACOTTA TILES IN THE VAULTED LIVING ROOM A MASSIVE SET OF PINE DOORS DATING FROM 1828 STANDS AS JOE'S TALISMAN. HE BOUGHT IT AFTER SUFFERING A HEART ATTACK, "WITH A PRAYER THAT I'D STILL BE AROUND TO PAINT IT". HE LEFT IT OUTSIDE FOR TEN YEARS, ALLOWING IT TO WEATHER, BEFORE TURNING IT INTO HIS LARGEST CANVAS. THE FRENCH GILTWOOD ARMCHAIR DATES FROM THE NINETEENTH CENTURY, UPHOLSTERED WITH CREAM AND BEIGE SILK FROM TASSINARI, A VENERABLE HOUSE THAT MADE FABRICS FOR MARIE ANTOINETTE AND CATHERINE DE MEDICI. THE HIGH-BACKED RUSH-BOTTOMED CHAIR IS PROVENÇAL, FROM THE EIGHTEENTH CENTURY.

HÔTEL DE LA MIRANDE

Few personal visions of Provence can be more heroic than that of Hannelore and Achim Stein, who, when they retired to the south of France, began a quest for something "interesting" to do. The result hides in a peaceful Avignon square, behind a mellow honey-colored façade that dates from 1688. The rest was created by the Steins from a jumble of houses of different eras, some predating the façade, but it is impossible to detect the joins. You believe that the Hôtel de la Mirande has stood in the shadow of the Palais des Papes for centuries, evolving imperceptibly over the years.

Their regard for authenticity was astonishing. With their son, Martin, the Steins made themselves experts on vernacular architecture by seeking out private houses in which original features had survived, combing through old records. They searched tirelessly for ancient floor-coverings, tiles and beams that they could acquire. When they finally began the transformation, instructors from the École d'Avignon—the only school in France that teaches traditional building methods—were brought in to show the *maçons* long-forgotten techniques: how to work with chalk-based paints, how to mix plaster that didn't come pre-prepared in bags.

The papers that line the walls of the bedrooms are precise historical copies of eighteenth-century handblocked wallpapers. Every pane of glass was handblown. The parquet floors, having been lifted from the ground floor strip by strip, and relaid upstairs in an identical pattern, literally creak with age.

The furnishings and fittings are eclectic, representing the centuries over which the hotel might have existed. In the principal dining room, for instance, a magnificent beamed and painted ceiling has survived from the fifteenth century; in one salon there are eighteenth-century Chinese wallpaper panels, painted for Western tastes; in the breakfast room nineteenth-century landscapes and scenes of Provençal life; in the private dining room a vast, glass-fronted *vitrine* made to house a collection of china given by Napoleon III to his godson.

When the Steins first opened their doors to the public in 1990, they were warned by more experienced hoteliers not to tempt their guests with beautiful things that might be damaged or stolen, but so far nothing has been lost. They see that as a reward for having created something timeless, something genuinely unique.

*A*BOVE LEFT: THE LIME GREEN
SHELVING, INSTALLED BY THE STEINS, WERE
HANDMADE BY PROVENÇAL CARPENTERS TO
A NEO-GOTHIC DESIGN THAT ECHOES THE
FAÇADE OF AVIGNON'S *PALAIS DES PAPES.*
BELOW LEFT: *FOUGASSE,* AND TWO ANTIQUE
BASKETS FROM THE HOTEL'S COLLECTION.
ABOVE: GLASS POTS OF THE HOTEL'S LAVEN-
DER HONEY, SERVED AT BREAKFAST.
RIGHT: WHEN A FORMER OWNER BECAME
MAYOR OF AVIGNON IN ABOUT 1850 HE IN-
STALLED THE CAST-IRON, WOOD-BURNING
COOKING RANGE IN WHAT WAS THEN A
TOWNHOUSE. ONE OF THE HOTEL'S TWO
KITCHENS, THIS IS USED FOR COOKERY
COURSES TAUGHT BY LOCAL CHEFS.

*L*EFT: AN EXACT COPY OF AN EIGHTEENTH-CENTURY COTTON PRINT, REPRODUCED BY LE MANACH, LINES THE WALLS OF THE HOTEL'S INTIMATE BAR, WHICH PROVIDES QUIET CORNERS FOR READING OR GAMES OF CHESS, AND DISCREET CONVERSATION. THE NINETEENTH-CENTURY ARMCHAIR HAS BEEN RE-COVERED IN FABRIC BY PIERRE FREY. THE CHESS PLAYERS' CHAIRS ARE ART DECO.

BELOW: A PLASTER DETAIL ABOVE THE HOTEL ENTRANCE, IN YELLOW OCHER, DATED 1688.

RIGHT: THE REFURBISHED SOFA IS COVERED IN FABRIC BY LE MANACH. PATTERNS REPRESENTING THE ZODIAC ARE INLAID ON THE SLATE TOP OF THE ROCOCO-STYLE TABLE.

*T*op and above: Georges's gypsy-style guinea-fowl is made with Provençal vegetables; for more exotic finds—sweet potatoes, plantain, Chinese cabbage—he visits markets in nearby Marseille.

Right: The coffee glasses on a drawer used to store metal type are "the simplest we could find".

Daydreaming in an ancient cobbled street in Avignon, Georges Laaland imagined the "harmony of cultures" he wanted to create, blending the culinary traditions of Provence with those of his native island of Guadeloupe, and of the Far East and Australia where he had spent many years traveling.

He intended to open a restaurant. The fact that he had no money was a problem, but he did have a name: Woolloomooloo, borrowed from a neighborhood in Sydney that was once a fabled spot for courting wallabies. He had also found just the right premises: an old printing shop, built over a picturesque canal in a quiet part of the original walled city.

Nothing much would be changed. The walls would remain coloured by age rather than paint. The huge printing forms, on which type had been cast, would provide his worktops, while the antiquated Linotype machine would be the striking center-piece. The cavernous space would be filled with plump, inviting sofas and whatever tables and chairs he could garner from junk shops. He would decorate the terrace according to the seasons, scattering, say, sand in the summer, leaves in the autumn. Then he would introduce his unique style of cuisine, mixing local ingredients with a riot of African spices, island flavors, and polyglot influences absorbed on his travels.

Unfortunately, as he quickly discovered, French health inspectors look askance at restaurant walls colored by age, and while there are government schemes to finance new businesses, it seemed to Georges that the money is only easily available for those who don't need it. Moreover, his prospective neighbors were none too happy, fearing that their ancient streets would be abuzz with African music and exotic smells.

Nevertheless, Georges was adamant that Woolloomooloo would open in time for Avignon's celebrated summer festival, and with a loan from a friend and the permission of a local court it did, in July 1993—albeit with the proviso that no food should be cooked on the premises until a health-inspector-approved kitchen was built. For the first six months Georges cooked in the kitchen of his apartment half-a-mile away, then miraculously carried the food to the restaurant on his head.

His perseverance paid off, so that now, in this pungent corner of Provence, the indigenous scents of thyme and lavender mix with those of coconut and lime—a vision of harmony vibrantly realized.

*L*EFT: A NINETEENTH-CENTURY JAPANESE CABINET BROUGHT BACK FROM FLORENCE ON TOP OF GEORGES'S CAR. HE FOUND THE GREEN-TOPPED TABLE IN A FLEA MARKET; IT CAME FROM A GRAND OLD RIVIERA HOTEL, THE SHELF BEING USED FOR THE HANDBAGS OF LADIES TAKING TEA.

BELOW: BOWLS FROM MOROCCO, USED FOR SERVING *HARIRA*, A TRADITIONAL SOUP EATEN AFTER SUNSET DURING RAMADAN.

RIGHT: A TYPE-CASTING MACHINE RESIDES IN THE CENTER OF THE RESTAURANT.

The patrician motor-yacht that sailed serenely into the Bay of Angels one fine spring morning in 1993, recalling the more elegant era of *The Great Gatsby*, was thinly disguised: the funnel was blue rather than yellow, the mast was shorter than it had once been, and she carried an unfamiliar name. Even so, to Claus Santon, a Danish naval architect and shipbuilder, watching from the balcony of his apartment overlooking the Old Port of Nice, her classic lines were hauntingly evocative. That Sunday evening Claus and his wife, Birgit, strolled along the quayside to where the yacht was moored, and, once close to, there was no further doubt in his mind. He knew that chance—or was it destiny?—had reunited him with "the loveliest motor-yacht I'd ever seen"—some twenty-five years before, in the Greek port of Piraeus.

She was built in Wales in 1930 with no regard for the cost of the materials: the hull was fashioned from teak—the most durable of woods—set on frames of sturdy oak, and the bottom was coppered. The planking, the decks and the whole of the deckhouse were also made of teak, while the saloon and the staterooms were lined with panels of Honduran mahogany. She was 110 feet long, from her clipper bow to her cruiser stern, and sumptuously equipped for long passages. The yachting press of the time had no hesitation in unanimously declaring that she was "indeed a fine ship".

More than sixty years later she was still a fine ship—though in need of some refurbishment—made all the more enticing by a fascinating history. President Franklin D. Roosevelt, it was said, had been a frequent guest on board, before she served the Royal Navy with distinction as a patrol vessel during the Second World War, after which she became the caprice of a Greek tycoon. When she arrived in Provence she was in search of a new owner, and, learning that, Claus and Birgit became determined to buy her.

Eighteen months later she was theirs, and with their children, Christoffer and Christine, and members of her crew, they set about restoring the engines and equipment—in fact every part of her. Virtually every inch of wood was taken back to its virgin state and coat after coat of ship's varnish was patiently reapplied.

Now, returned to her original splendor, she sails the Provençal coast on charter (with a crew of six, including a gourmet chef) proudly bearing the name that perfectly describes her: *Classique*.

*L*EFT: A CASUAL DINING TABLE, SET UNDER AN AWNING ON THE *CLASSIQUE'S* SPACIOUS TEAK DECKS, EVOKES DAYDREAMS OF LAZY SUMMER MEALS AT SEA.
TOP AND ABOVE: THE FUNNEL AND WHEEL-HOUSE, LIKE EVERYTHING ELSE ON THE BOAT, WERE BOTH CAREFULLY RESTORED.

𝓛EFT: IN HALCYON WEATHER THE *CLASSIQUE* GLIDES SERENELY OUT TO SEA. RIGHT: FOR MORE FORMAL OCCASIONS THE MAIN DINING SALOON, WITH ITS MAGNIFICENT ORIGINAL MAHOGANY PANELS AND FURNISHINGS, CONJURES UP MEMORIES OF A BYGONE ERA.

Guide

*W*hat
follows is not meant to be a comprehensive guide to Provence;

rather it is an idiosyncratic list of places and establishments

Sølvi Dos Santos enjoyed while working on this book.

Unless otherwise stated, the hotels, restaurants and cafés are

reasonably priced. Be warned: most restaurants

in France are closed on at least one day a week, and many restaurants

and hotels close for a month or more out of season.

It is always advisable to telephone in advance to check opening times.

Aix-en-Provence

HOTELS

Hôtel des Quatre Dauphins
54 rue Roux-Alphéran
Tel: 42 38 16 39 Fax: 42 38 60 19
Small, colorful and charming, and
located in the heart of Aix.

Le Manoir
8 rue d'Entrecasteaux
Tel: 42 26 27 20 Fax: 42 27 17 97
Once a fourteenth-century cloister,
this quiet jewel is also found in the
center of the city.

Villa Gallici
Traverse du Castellet, Avenue de la
Violette
Tel: 42 23 29 23 Fax: 42 96 30 45
With an ambience more like a family
house than a hotel, the villa is set in a
pretty garden, and you can eat on the
terrace under plane trees. Rather
expensive.

RESTAURANTS AND CAFÉS

Brasserie Le Verdun
20 place Verdun
Tel: 42 27 03 24
A pleasant bistro with a terrace,
overlooking a small flea market.

Gu et Fils
3 rue Frédéric-Mistral
Tel: 42 26 75 12
A popular venue serving sophisticated
dishes.

Les Deux Garçons
53 cours Mirabeau
Tel: 42 26 00 51
The city's most famous terrace; the
place to be seen.

Le Clos de la Violette
10 avenue de la Violette
Tel: 42 23 30 71
Surrounded by a beautiful garden.
Serves sophisticated food at medium
to high prices.

MARKETS

Vegetable market: Place de la
Madeleine, on Tuesday, Thursday and
Saturday mornings.

Flea market: Place du Palais-de-
Justice, on Tuesday, Thursday and
Saturday mornings.

Flower markets: Place de la Mairie, on
Tuesday, Thursday and Saturday
mornings. On Sunday morning the
market moves to the place de la
Madeleine.

SHOPS

Carocim
Quartier Beaufort, Puyricard
Tel: 42 92 20 39
Offers glorious handmade cement tiles
in a wide array of patterns and
colours. Open Monday to Friday.

Antibes

RESTAURANTS

Le Transat
17 avenue du 11 Novembre
Tel: 93 34 20 20
Close to the yachting harbor and the
entrance to the old town.

MARKETS

Fruit, vegetable and fish market: Place
Masséna, every morning except
Monday.

Flea/antiques market: Place Audiverti,
on Thursday and Saturday, from 7am
to 6pm.

Apt

RESTAURANTS

Restaurant Bernard Mathys
Route national 100, 4km west of Apt
Tel: 90 04 84 64
Located in an eighteenth-century
bastide surrounded by a large park.
The menu changes with the seasons.

MARKETS

Vegetable market: throughout the
center of the old town, on Tuesday
and Saturday mornings.

Pottery market: on Tuesday in July
and August.

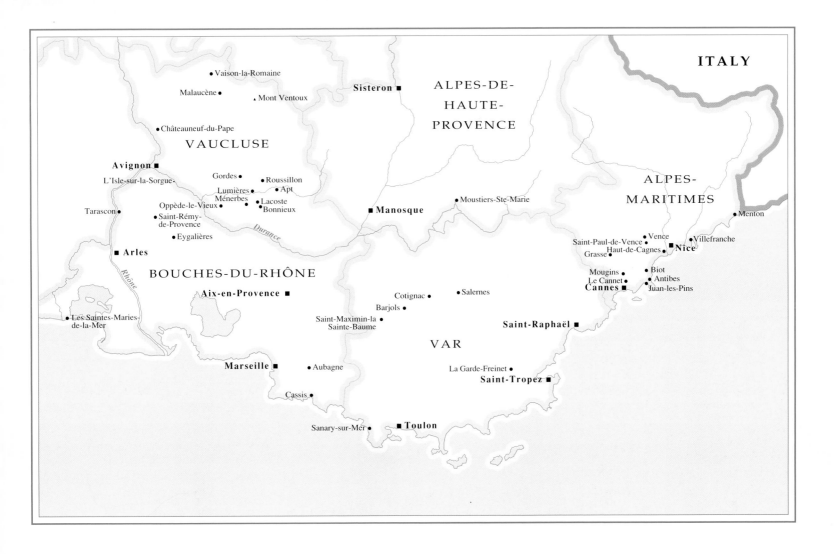

SHOPS

Société des Ocres de France
Impasse des Ocriers
Tel: 90 74 63 82
Sells natural pigments from the
Roussillon area.

Arles

HOTELS

Le Calendal
22 place du Docteur Pomme
Tel: 90 96 11 89 Fax: 90 96 05 84
Next to the Roman arches and
recently redecorated. The garden is
charming.

Grand Hôtel Nord-Pinus
Place du Forum
Tel: 90 93 44 44 Fax: 90 93 34 00
The bullfighters' favorite rendezvous,
now glamorously restored (see page
61).

RESTAURANTS AND CAFÉS

Café Van Gogh
Place du Forum
Tel: 90 96 44 56
Across from the Grand Hôtel Nord-
Pinus, the café is named after one of
Arles's best-known visitors.

L'Affenage
4 rue Molière
Tel: 90 96 07 67
Located in what was a post office
during the eighteenth century, this is
the Arlesians' favorite "canteen".
A glowing fire in the large fireplace
creates a cosy atmosphere.

MARKETS

Vegetable market: Boulevard Émile-
Combes on Wednesday morning,
Boulevard des Lices on Saturday
morning.

Flea market: Boulevard des Lices, on
the first Wednesday of the month.

SHOPS

Boutique Christian Lacroix
52 rue de la République
Tel: 90 96 11 16
A dazzling space, sparkling with the
designer's clothes and jewelery
(see page 61).

FESTIVALS

La Pegoulada
On the first Sunday of July a
torchlight procession through the
town celebrates the beauty and
traditions of the Camargue. The
festivities last from sundown to the
small hours of the morning,
culminating in a pageant of music and
dance in the Roman Arena.

Avignon

HOTELS

Hôtel de la Mirande
4 place de la Mirande
Tel: 90 85 93 93 Fax: 90 86 26 85
An exquisitely created illusion of the
past. Expensive but exceptional
(see page 180).

Palais des Papes
1 rue Gérard Philippe
Tel: 90 82 47 31 Fax: 90 27 91 17
In the heart of the original walled city,
with prettily-decorated bedrooms that
add to its charm.

La Ferme Jamet
Ile de la Barthelasse
Tel: 90 86 16 74 Fax: 90 86 17 72
A former farm, now a bed and
breakfast, on a tranquil island in the
middle of the Rhône.

RESTAURANTS

Woolloomooloo
16 bis rue des Teinturiers
Tel: 90 85 28 44
Housed in an old printing shop, with a
terrace overlooking an ancient cobbled
street. The food is influenced by the
owner's exotic travels (see page 186).

Le Bain Marie
5 rue Pétramale
Tel: 90 85 21 37
Delicious food. On fine days served at
tables set out in an ancient courtyard.

SHOPS

Globe Trotter
28 place Change
Tel: 90 82 01 42
Warm-toned furniture, tiles and items for the home with a Southern flavor (see page 82).

MARKETS

Indoor vegetable market: Les Halles, place Pie, open before dawn every morning except Monday.

Flea markets: Place Crillon on Saturday morning, Place des Carmes on Sunday morning.

FESTIVALS

Festival d'Avignon: Throughout July and August; renowned for its wide and varied dance and theatre program.

Biot

HOTELS

Galerie des Arcades
16 place des Arcades
Tel: 93 65 01 04 Fax: 93 65 01 05
Dramatically set in a former fifteenth-century cloister, with a family-run restaurant serving homemade specialities.

Bonnieux

RESTAURANTS

Le Fournil
Place Carnot
Tel: 90 75 83 62
Intimate and rustic, serving typical Provençal dishes. Overlooks a seventeenth-century fountain in the town's most picturesque square.

Auberge de la Loube
Buoux village, 6 miles from Bonnieux
Tel: 90 74 19 58
A former farm that is now a restaurant, in a remote and dramatic setting.

SHOPS

Au Chocolat Chaud
7 rue de la République
The town's renowned baker also offers delicious confectionery.

MARKETS

Vegetable market: town center, on Friday morning.

Camargue

FESTIVALS

Les Saintes-Maries-de-la-Mer
Each July the six-day Festival of the Horse brings together more than a dozen different breeds of Camargue horses. The festivities include equestrian competitions, held in the Saintes-Maries arena.

Cannes

RESTAURANTS

La Patinière du Palais
13 square Mérimée
Tel: 93 39 02 82
Located opposite the Palais des Festivals, with a small terrace for summer dining.

Le Relais à Mougins
Place de la Mairie, Mougins-Village
Tel: 93 90 03 47
Refined cuisine, and a splendid spot for people-watching on warm summer evenings.

MARKETS

Vegetable market: Quartier Fouville, every day except Monday, from 7am to 1pm.

Flea markets: Quartier Fouville, on Monday (October to June, from 8am to 6pm, and July to September, from 3pm to 10pm), Place de la Poste, in the Quartier La Bocca, on Thursday morning.

Cassis

HOTEL

Hôtel les Roches Blanches
Route des Calanques
Tel: 42 01 09 30 Fax: 42 01 94 23
A nineteenth-century house, recently restored, this small hotel has a private beach and a breathtaking view of the sea.

RESTAURANTS

Chez Gilbert
19 quai des Baux
Tel: 42 01 71 36
Specializing in fish, with a lively terrace set by the harbour.

MARKETS

Fish and vegetable market: on Wednesday and Friday mornings.

Cotignac

HOTELS

Hostellerie Provençale "Lou Calen"
1 cours Gambetta
Tel: 94 04 60 40 Fax: 94 04 76 64
Filled with old-fashioned charm, and boasting a renowned restaurant that serves traditional dishes—in the garden during the summer months.

RESTAURANTS

Le Restaurant des Sports
Cours Gambetta
Tel: 94 04 60 17
In the center of Cotignac, shaded by plane trees. Closed during the winter.

MARKETS

Vegetable market: on Tuesday morning.

Eygalières

HOTELS

L'Auberge Provençal
Place de la Mairie
Tel: 90 95 91 00 Fax: 90 95 60 92
An eighteenth-century post office, now a charming hotel with a welcoming fireplace and a fine restaurant.

Le Mas de l'Ange
Petite route de St-Rémy, Mollégès
Tel: 90 95 08 33 Fax: 90 95 48 69
A delightfully decorated bed and breakfast in a farmhouse with a marvelous view of Les Alpilles (see page 14).

RESTAURANTS

Sous les Micocouliers
Traverse Montfort
Tel: 90 95 94 53
Cosy inside in the winter, with a terrace shaded by nettle trees for long summer lunches. Inventive Provençal food.

MARKETS

Vegetable market: on Friday morning.

Gordes

HOTELS

Le Renaissance
Place du Château
Tel: 90 72 02 02 Fax: 90 72 05 11
A family-run hotel in the center of this well-known Lubéron village, with bedrooms that are spacious and nicely decorated. The restaurant is well worth a visit.

La Ferme de la Huppe
Les Pourquiers
Route départementale 156
Tel: 90 72 12 25
An inviting haven nestling in the
countryside below the village.

MARKETS

Vegetable market: on Tuesday
morning.

Goult

SHOPS

Edith Mézard
Château de l'Ange, Lumières
Tel: 90 72 36 41
Edith sells her gorgeous embroidered
fabrics in the former stables of her
home (see page 43).

Haut-de-Cagnes

HOTELS

Le Grimaldi
6 place du Château
Tel: 93 20 60 24 Fax: 92 02 19 47
Situated at the summit of this old
hilltop village, next to the château-
museum. A cosy place to eat on
winter days.

Lacoste

HOTELS

La Bonne Terre
Route de Saint Véran
Tel and Fax: 90 75 85 53
A bed and breakfast on the outskirts
of the village, with spectacular views
of the Lubéron. The rooms are
attractive, and there is a swimming
pool in the grounds.

RESTAURANTS

Restaurant le Loofoc
Rue Basse
Tel: 90 75 89 76
Simple but honest food, with views of
the neighboring village of Bonnieux
from the terrace.

MARKETS

Vegetable market: on Tuesday
morning.

L'Isle-sur-la-Sorgue

HOTELS

Mas de Cure Bourse
Route de Caumont-sur-Durance
Tel: 90 38 16 58 Fax: 90 38 52 31
Surrounded by vineyards, this
restored farmhouse now offers
comfortable rooms and a
recommended restaurant.

RESTAURANTS

Le Jardin du Quai
4 avenue "Julien Guigue"
Tel: 90 38 56 17
Conveniently opposite the railway
station, with a shady garden for
summer eating.

Lou Nego Chin
12 quai Jean Jaurès
Tel: 90 20 88 03
Boasts a terrace overlooking the River
Sorgue; a cool refuge from the bustle
of the markets.

MARKETS

Vegetable market: throughout the
town center, on Thursday and Sunday
mornings.

Flea/antiques market: Avenue des
Quatre Otages, on Saturday and
Sunday.

SHOPS

Michel Biehn
7 avenue des Quatre Otages
Tel: 90 20 89 04
A collection of wonderful things to
buy, as eclectic as the man himself
(see page 75).

Xavier Nicod
9 avenue des Quatre Otages
Tel: 90 38 07 20
An Aladdin's Cave of antiques
(see page 54).

Aux Deux Soeurs
7 place de la Liberté
Tel: 90 38 11 32
A captivating mixture of furniture, china, glass and exotic textiles, housed in an airy space in the town centre (see page 112).

Lorgues

Chez Bruno
Quartier le Plan,
Campagne Mariette
Tel: 94 73 92 19
Bruno is the "Truffle King". His truffle dishes are expensive but worth the price.

Malaucène

MAIL ORDER

Brigitte Delebecque
84340 Malaucène
Tel: 90 65 17 30 Fax: 90 65 16 66
Brigitte will supply details of her products by mail or fax, and will ship them all over the world (see page 78).

Marseille

RESTAURANTS

Café des Arts
122 rue du Vallon des Auffes
Tel: 91 31 51 64
Set in a beautiful courtyard painted in warm Provençal colours.

Bar de la Marine
15 quai Rive Neuve
Tel: 91 54 95 47
One of Pagnol's favorite harborside haunts.

Brasserie New York
33 quai des Belges
Tel: 91 33 91 79
A café and brasserie that is a meeting place for artists and journalists.

MARKETS

Fish market: Quai des Belges, every morning.
Flea market: Cours Julien, on the second Sunday of the month. Les Pièces, on Friday, Saturday and Sunday.

Ménerbes

SHOPS

Sacha Antiquités Décoration
Place Albert Roure
Tel: 90 72 41 28
A treasure trove of unusual antiques, and a tempting array of decorative items for the home (see page 36).

Menton

RESTAURANTS

Le Grand Bleu
1684 promenade du Soleil
Tel: 93 57 46 33
Aptly named, for its epithet describes both the dominant colour of the decor and that of the sea that it overlooks.

Moustiers-Sainte-Marie

HOTELS

La Bastide de Moustiers
La Grisolière
Tel: 92 70 47 47 Fax: 92 70 47 48
Expensive, but the décor is superb. Worth the sacrifice.

MARKETS

Vegetable market: on Friday morning.

Nice

HOTELS

Hôtel Windsor
11 rue Dalpozzo
Tel: 93 88 59 35
Fax: 93 88 94 57
Large rooms look out on to a beautiful garden.

Hôtel Mercure
91 quai des États-Unis
Tel: 93 85 74 19
Fax: 93 13 90 94
A comfortable modern hotel near the restaurants and markets of the Old Town, and looking on to the Promenade des Anglais.

RESTAURANTS

Le Safari
1 cours Saleya
Tel: 93 80 18 44
Ideal for lunch or dinner all year round. In the Old Town, in the midst of the flower market.

Le Rive Droite
22 avenue Saint Jean Baptiste
Tel: 93 62 16 72
Nominated 'Best Traditional Restaurant' by a jury of French journalists.

MARKETS

Flower and vegetable market: Cours Saleya, every morning except Monday.

Flea market: Cours Saleya, every Monday, from 8am to 5pm.

Saint-Paul-de-Vence

HOTELS

La Colombe d'Or
1 Place Général de Gaulle
Tel: 93 32 80 02 Fax: 93 32 77 78
Flaunts the prettiest—and best-known—dining terrace in the south of France. Inside, the walls are hung with pictures donated by the artists who have stayed there or visited. An institution.

Saint-Rémy-de-Provence

HOTELS

Les Antiques
15 avenue Pasteur
Tel: 90 92 03 02
Fax: 90 92 50 40
A charming eighteenth-century house set in a large garden, offering a sojourn in the past.

Hôtel Ville Verte
18 place de la République
Tel: 90 92 06 14 Fax: 90 92 56 54
A friendly family-owned hotel located in the center of the town. Excellent value for money. Both rooms and studios are available, and there is a swimming pool.

RESTAURANTS

Le Bistrot des Alpilles
15 boulevard Mirabeau
Tel: 90 92 09 17
Friendly, bustling bistro atmosphere.

MARKETS

Vegetable market: on Wednesday and Saturday mornings.

Saint-Tropez

HOTELS

Hôtel Sube
15 quai Suffren
Tel: 94 97 30 04 Fax: 94 54 89 08
In the heart of the Côte d'Azur's most fashionable town, overlooking the picturesque harbour.

CAFÉS

Café de Paris
Tel: 94 97 00 56
On the ground floor of the Hôtel Sube, but separately owned. A simple, cosy bistro.

MARKETS

Vegetable market: on Tuesday and Saturday mornings.

Flea market: on Saturday morning.

Sanary-sur-Mer

HOTELS

Roc Amour
Boulevard de la Falaise
Tel: 94 74 13 54 Fax: 94 74 03 42
Peacefully hidden in a residential area
by the sea.

Hôtel de la Tour
24 quai Général de Gaulle
Tel: 94 74 10 10 Fax: 94 74 69 49
Centrally located on the waterfront,
with a large terrace and a restaurant
that specializes in fish.

RESTAURANTS

L'en K
4 rue Louis Blanc
Tel: 94 74 66 57
In one of the town's narrow streets, it
rejoices in sophisticated dishes and
large portions.

El Dogo
11 rue Laget
Tel: 94 74 58 80
An Argentinian restaurant with
colorful dishes and an interior to
match.

SHOPS

L'Atelier du Sud
23 rue Félix Pijeaud
Tel: 94 88 35 88
A furnishing store that displays
mosaic items made by LuluBerlu.

LuluBerlu
132 allée Anna, Villa St Jean
Tel: 94 88 29 49 Fax: 94 88 28 19
This is the partners' home and
showroom. They offer a mail-order
service, or can supply a list of shops
that sell their designs (see page 69).

Tarascon

SHOPS

Souleiado
Musée Charles Deméry
39 rue Proudhon
Tel: 90 91 08 80
After touring the fascinating museum
you can visit the shop, which sells the
famous printed-fabric items (see page
62).

Vaison-la-Romaine

HOTELS

Hostellerie le Beffroi
Rue de l'Évêché, Cité Médiévale
Tel: 90 36 04 71 Fax: 90 36 24 78
Each bedroom is different, decorated
with antique furniture and paintings.
The hotel, which dates from the
sixteenth century, boasts its own
restaurant, 'La Fontaine'.

RESTAURANTS

Le Bateleur
1 place Théodore Aubanel
Tel: 90 36 28 04
A family-run restaurant serving
traditional cuisine.

MARKETS

Vegetable market: on Tuesday
morning.

Villefranche-sur-Mer

HOTELS

Hôtel Welcome
1 quai Courbet
Tel: 93 76 76 93 Fax: 93 01 88 81
Set on the seafront, overlooking the
fishing boats in a charming harbour,
with views of Cap Ferrat. Opposite is
a chapel where Cocteau painted
frescoes.

YACHT CHARTER

Classique
2 avenue Albert I
Tel: 93 01 75 55 Fax 93 01 73 40
(See page 191).

MARKETS

Flea market: Port de la Santé, on
Sunday and national holidays, from
9am to 5pm.

INDEX

Page numbers in bold refer to entries in the Guide.

A

Aix-en-Provence, 75, 78, **196**
Ambrose, Laurence and David, 130–35
Antibes, **196**
Apt, 98, **196**
Arles, 30, 61, 74, 78, **198**
Avignon, 62, 82, 180, 186, **198**

B

Beaucaire, 62
BED AND BREAKFAST
　La Ferme Jamet, Avignon, **198**
　Le Mas de l'Ange, near Eygalières, 14, **200**
Biehn, Michel, 75–77, **202**
Biot, **199**
Bonnieux, **199**

C

CAFÉS
　Bar de la Manne, Marseille, **202**
　Café de Paris, St-Tropez, **203**
　Café des Arts, Marseille, **202**
　Café Van Gogh, Arles, **198**
　Les Deux Garçons, Aix, **196**
Camargue, **199**
Cannes, **199**
Cassis, **200**
Castanier, Marie-Stella, 82–87, **199**
Cavaillon, 14, 78
Classique, 191, **204**
Conran, Sir Terence, 153–57
Corre, Marine, 112–15, **202**
Cotignac, **200**

D

de Vésian, Nicole, 48–53
Degrelle, Charlie, 69, **204**

Delebecque, Brigitte, 78–81, **202**
Deméry, Charles, 62
Downing, Joe, 174–79

E

Eygalières, **202**

F

FESTIVALS
　Arles, **198**
　Avignon, **199**
　Les Saintes-Maries-de-la-Mer, **199**
Fournier, Joel, 88

G

Gessel, Michael van, 141–43
Gordes, **200**
Goult, **201**
Grange, Jacques, 30–35

H

Haut-de-Cagnes, **201**
HOTELS
　Auberge Provençal, Eygalières, **200**
　Bonne Terre, Lacoste, **201**
　Ferme de la Huppe, near Gordes, **201**
　Galerie des Arcades, Biot, **199**
　Grand Hôtel Nord-Pinus, Arles, 61, **198**
　Hostellerie le Beffroi, Vaison, **204**
　Hostellerie Provençale Lou Calen, Cotignac, **200**
　Hôtel de la Mirande, Avignon, 180, **198**
　Hôtel de la Tour, Sanary-sur-Mer, **204**
　Hôtel des Quatre Dauphins, Aix, **196**
　Hôtel les Roches Blanches, Cassis, **200**
　Hôtel Mercure, Nice, **203**
　Hôtel Sube, St-Tropez, **203**
　Hôtel Ville Verte, St-Rémy, **203**
　Hôtel Welcome, Villefranche-sur-Mer, **204**
　Hôtel Windsor, Nice, **202**
　La Bastide de Moustiers, Moustiers-

Sainte-Marie, **202**
　La Colombe d'Or, Saint-Paul-de-Vence, **203**
　Le Calendal, Arles, **198**
　Le Grimaldi, Haut-de-Cagnes, **201**
　Le Manoir, Aix, **196**
　Le Renaissance, Gordes, **200**
　Les Antiques, St-Rémy, **203**
　Mas de Cure Bourse, L'Isle, **201**
　Palais des Papes, Avignon, **198**
　Roc Amour, Sanary-sur-Mer, **204**
　Villa Gallici, Aix, **196**
Houant, Sacha and Lionel, 36–41, **202**
Hunter, James, 112–15
Hyères, 69

I

Igou, Anne, 61

J

Jourdan, Marie, 158–65

K

Klein, Michel, 88–97

L

L'Isle-sur-la-Sorgue, 54, 75, 112, **201**
la Falaise, Maxime de, 107
La Seyne, 68
Laaland, Georges, 186–89, **198**
Lacoste, **201**
Lacroix, Christian, 61, **198**
Lafforgue, Hélène and Bruno, 14–21, **200**
Le Lavandou, 69
LuluBerlu, 69–73, **204**
Lumières, 42

M

MAIL ORDER
　Brigitte Delebecque, Malaucène, 78, **202**

MARKETS
    Aix-en-Provence, **196**
    Antibes, **196**
    Apt, **196**
    Arles, **198**
    Avignon, **199**
    Bonnieux, **199**
    Cannes, **199**
    Cassis, **200**
    Cotignac, **200**
    Eygalières, **200**
    Gordes, **201**
    L'Isle-sur-la-Sorgue, **201**
    Lacoste, **201**
    Marseille, **202**
    Moustiers-Sainte-Marie, **202**
    Nice, **202**, **203**
    Saint-Tropez, **203**
    St-Rémy-de-Provence, **203**
    Vaison-la-Romaine, **204**
    Villefranche-sur-Mer, **204**
Marseille, **202**
Maussane, 78
Ménerbes, 36, **202**
Menton, 122, **202**
Mézard, Edith, 43–47, **201**
Moustiers-Sainte-Marie, **202**

N

Nall, 116–21
Nice, 191, **202**
Nicod, Xavier, 54–59, **202**
Nokin, Natacha, 69, **204**

O

Olney, Richard, 136–39

P

Pronk, Cees, 141–43

R

RESTAURANTS
    Auberge de la Loube, Bonnieux, **199**
    Brasserie Le Verdun, Aix, **196**
    Chez Bruno, Lacoste, **201**
    Chez Gilbert, Cassis, **200**
    Chez Gu (Gu et Fils), Aix, **196**
    El Dogo, Sanary-sur-Mer, **204**
    L'Affenage, Arles, **198**
    L'en K, Sanary-sur-Mer, **204**
    La Patinière du Palais, Cannes, **199**
    Le Bain Marie, Avignon, **198**
    Le Bateleur, Vaison, **204**
    Le Bistrot des Alpilles, St-Rémy, **203**
    Le Clos de la Violette, Aix, **196**
    Le Fournil, Bonnieux, **199**
    Le Grand Bleu, Menton, **202**
    Le Jardin du Quai, L'Isle, **201**
    Le New York, Marseille, **202**
    Le Relais à Mougins, near Cannes, **199**
    Le Restaurant des Sports, Cotignac, **200**
    Le Rive Droite, Nice, **203**
    Le Safari, Nice, **203**
    Le Transat, Antibes, **196**
    Lou Nego Chin, L'Isle, **201**
    Restaurant Bernard Mathys, Apt, **196**
    Restaurant Loofoc, Lacoste, **201**
    Sous les Micocouliers, Eygalières, **200**
    Woolloomooloo, Avignon, 186, **198**
Richerenches, 78

S

Saint-Paul-de-Vence, **203**
Saint-Rémy-de-Provence, **203**
Saint-Tropez, **203**
Sanary-sur-Mer, 69, **204**
Santon, Claus, 191–92, **204**
Schipper, Arjan, 141–43
SHOPS
    Au Chocolat Chaud, Bonnieux, **199**
    Aux Deux Soeurs, L'Isle, 112, **202**

Boutique Christian Lacroix, Arles, 60, **198**
Carocim, near Aix, **196**
Edith Mézard, near Goult, 43, **201**
Globe Trotter, Avignon, 82, **199**
L'Atelier du Sud, Sanary-sur-Mer, **204**
LuluBerlu, Sanary-sur-Mer, 69, **204**
Michel Biehn, L'Isle, 75, **202**
Sacha Antiquités Décoration, Ménerbes, 36, **202**
Société des Ocres de France, Apt, **198**
Souleiado, Tarascon, 62, **204**
Xavier Nicod, L'Isle, 54, **202**
Silvagni, Irène and Giorgio, 22–29
Souleiado, 62–67, **204**
St George, Sarah, 107–11
Stein, Hannelore and Achim, 180, **198**
Stein, Martin, 180, **198**

T

Tarascon, 62, **204**
Toulon, 136

V

Vaison-la-Romaine, 78, **204**
Valréas, 78
Vartan, Tania, 126–29
Vence, 116
Villefranche-sur-Mer, **204**

W

Warren, Catharine, 167–73
Waterfield, William, 122–25
Wells, Patricia and Walter, 98–105
Williams, Lillian and Ted, 144–51

Y

YACHT CHARTER
    Claus Santon, 191, **204**

ACKNOWLEDGEMENTS

We wish to offer heartfelt thanks to all those who so graciously opened their doors to us and allowed us to photograph and record their private worlds.

Sølvi Dos Santos would also like to thank her friends who offered constant encouragement and her family: her mother for her patient presence during this project and her daughter Camila.

Sara Walden wishes to thank Gwen Clark, Karen Fawcett, Tony Rocca, Lotte and Philip Jarvis, Elizabeth Kime, John Bastable, Sacha and Lionel Houant and, especially, Philippe and Marlies de Font-Réaulx and Philippe Guezel. Sue Bastable's steadfast support went far beyond what was asked of her. Paul Eddy did more than he will ever know.

The publisher would like to thank Barbara Mellor for her contribution towards the Introduction, and Libby Willis for her patient editing.

Published in 1996 and distributed in the U.S. by
Stewart, Tabori & Chang
a division of U.S. Media Holdings, Inc.
575 Broadway, New York, NY 10012

Distributed in Canada by General Publishing Co., Ltd.,
30 Lesmill Road, Don Mills, Ontario, Canada M3B 2T6
Distributed in Europe by Onslow Books, Ltd.
Tyler's Court, 111A Wardour Street, London W1V 3TD, England

First published in Great Britain in 1996 by
Conran Octopus Limited, London, England
Copyright © J. W. Cappelens Forlag A. S.

Library of Congress Catalog Card Number 95-72931.

ISBN: 1-55670-449-6

Editorial Directors: Tove Storsveen/Suzannah Gough
Editorial Assistant: Helen Green
Designer: Marc Walter

Printed in Italy

1 3 5 7 9 8 6 4 2

First Edition